8-10-02

To my Brother,

Enjoy reading about the heroes of Gladiator life. We are thankful for your presence in our family. In a way, you are our

"GLADIATOR!"

Vincus

Derinitus

Williamus !!

Strength & Honor

Happy Birthday
From the Knotts Family

THE
GLADIATOR

THE

GLADIATOR

THE SECRET HISTORY OF ROME'S WARRIOR SLAVES

ALAN BAKER

THOMAS DUNNE BOOKS
St. Martin's Press New York

THOMAS DUNNE BOOKS.
An imprint of St. Martin's Press.

www.stmartins.com

ISBN 0-312-28403-9

First published in Great Britain by Ebury Press
Random House UK Limited

10 9 8 7 6 5 4 3 2

This book is for Paul Hughes,
for many years of friendship.

Contents

Introduction

The ancient Romans loved gladiators. They loved the men, the weapons, the fighting and the bloodshed. They also loved the death. Bathed in the fierce heat of the Mediterranean sun, the Romans rejoiced in the blood of the dead and the dying, for in so doing they showed the qualities that had made their civilisation great and powerful. They demonstrated their utter contempt for suffering and death.

The great amphitheatres of Rome and her provinces were routinely packed with spectators, who watched men fight bloody battles, both with each other and with a dazzling array of wild and dangerous animals. Awful violence stalked the arenas in the form of sword, arrow, trident, tooth and claw, of an intensity that we can barely now imagine. In fact, as we shall see, the man-to-man combats themselves, in which countless thousands of men died, were by no means the most bloodthirsty events on show. In later years they were preceded by the wild animal hunts where men fought with ferocious beasts, often winning, but sometimes being torn to pieces. The arena was also a place of public executions, where men and women were thrown defenceless to the beasts. Their excruciating suffering brought forth cheers and applause from the spectators; to be horrified or even mildly upset by such sights was considered a pitiful and un-Roman weakness.

The gladiators themselves were the superstars of their day, lusted after by both women and men. Their celebrity status ensured that they were followed by crowds of adoring fans whenever they went out into the streets. At the same time, the nature of their profession all but ensured a horribly violent end. While some gladiators became wealthy on the prizes given to them after a victory and were able to enjoy a comfortable retirement, most did not live long enough and met their deaths in a vast expanse of hot, gore-stained sand, the roar of the blood in their ears drowned out by the screams of the crowd.

And yet in a curious paradox that lies at the heart of the secret history of gladiators, what the crowd loved they also held in the greatest contempt. The Roman people looked down on their gladiators even as they cheered their triumphs and howled abuse at their defeats.

Their enjoyment of the spectacle, however, is not disputed. The vast majority of people today would doubtless turn away in utter horror from the events of the arena. To watch a man or woman being ripped apart or eaten alive by a wild beast would be too much to bear even once, let alone for a whole day, or even many days. Nevertheless, what the historian Michael Grant has called 'the nastiest blood-sport ever invented' was much loved in ancient Rome, and it remains one of the most troubling aspects of a culture that bequeathed to the world so much that is noble and beautiful.

But at the same time, it is a serious mistake to consider these spectacles purely in the context of modern morality. To apply our own values to a civilisation two thousand years removed in history is absurd, and will certainly not help us to understand the games or the reasons for their development. In our own age, human life is prized and respected above all else (at least in theory); to inflict suffering on others for the sake of enjoyment is considered perverse and incomprehensible. But such a perspective simply did not exist in the ancient world. The morality of the Roman state was more complex. They avoided pointless cruelty whenever possible, and nowhere more strikingly than in their treatment of vanquished nations. Revenge was not something to which the Romans surrendered easily. Instead, they calculated that treating their defeated enemies well would avoid stoking up the sort of trouble that would interfere with the profitable running of the new province. They massacred people to be sure, and brought many prisoners of war to meet their deaths in the arena, but this tended to be a last resort, a means of dealing finally with an irreconcilable foe.

The punishments meted out before the spectators, which included the most awful tortures, were dreadful and cruel to a truly extraordinary degree – but they were not arbitrary. They were performed for specific reasons, based on the nature of the crime committed and on the level of suffering caused to the victim of the crime.

Although we should view the events of the arena free of modern preconceptions, it is interesting nonetheless to trace the legacy of the games in our own time. Most of us follow pursuits that have clear antecedents in the gladiatorial shows of antiquity. In an echo of the wild beast hunts of the arena, people in Britain still don special clothes and ostentatiously hunt the fox. Our own sportsmen, too, are merely the pale echoes of the ancient fighters; our fencers use blunt rapiers instead of swords and tridents, and serious injuries are rare. Our footballers, rugby players and tennis players display their skill and aggression before thousands of screaming spectators, with millions more watching on television. When a football match is over, it is not entirely unknown for the teams' supporters to take to the streets and engage in battles with each other. Injuries and deaths occur, and those who consider themselves civilised bemoan the violence and bloodshed. This is exactly what happened in the ancient world: on the days when games were held, fans from rival towns would hurl abuse at each other, write insulting graffiti on walls, a flashpoint would be reached and the violence would commence.

As for the Roman love of violence, we cannot, in all honesty, make any serious claim that our own culture really abhors violence. As more than one commentator on the ancient world has noted, modern society still feels the need to watch violent events, whether they be at a boxing match or spattered across the cinema screen. The wars we wage (whether for good reasons or bad) have become another branch of the entertainment industry, thanks to the ubiquity of electronic media, which includes cameras attached to the nose-cones of rockets. We should therefore ask ourselves how easy it is to condemn ancient societies such as Rome for their cruelty, when our own politicians blandly justify the bombing and incineration of innocent civilians in other countries, or profit from the sale of weapons to repressive regimes abroad.

This book, therefore, is an attempt to chart the history of the Roman games without succumbing to the anachronism of imposing our own early twenty-first-century moral attitudes upon them. We will explore the terrifying world of the glad-iators and gladiatorial combats, from their origins as violent rituals honouring the dead, to their final abolition almost a thousand years later. While the images most closely associated with gladiators are those of two men battling to the death or a defenceless Christian being eaten by lions, there are many more elements for us to consider. The games were not merely frivo-lous entertainments, consumed by mindless plebeians: they played a central role in the political and cultural life of Rome. We will examine the various forms of combat, from gladiatorial arms and fighting styles to the incredibly elaborate entertain-ments provided in the naval battles. We will look, also, at the dramatic re-enactments, in which condemned criminals were forced to act out the parts of various doomed characters from Greco-Roman mythology.

The origin of the amphitheatre, one of the most recognisable and magnificent architectural forms of the ancient world, will be described, as will the infrequent but significant practice of Emperors, such as Caligula and Commodus, actually fighting as gladiators. Chapter Twelve, entitled 'A Day at the Games', might be described as the book's centre-piece: its intention is to provide the reader with, I hope, an atmospheric view of a day spent at a gladiatorial event.

Since this book is intended as a popular account of gladiatorial combats, rather than an academic or scholarly study, I have not included numbered footnotes in the text. There is a bibliography and further reading list for those readers wishing to pursue a closer study of this fascinating and disturbing aspect of ancient history.

BEGINNINGS

Hundreds of thousands of people were sent to their deaths in the amphitheatres of ancient Rome, whether through battling with each other or being forced to bear themselves to the onslaughts of wild animals. We can barely imagine the agonies of condemned criminals and slaves, abandoned to the teeth and claws of carnivorous beasts, their quivering bodies bitten, slashed and dragged across the blood-soaked sand of the arena to the approving cheers of the assembled Roman masses. What unspeakable terrors must have accompanied the final minutes of the life of a prisoner of war goaded into the arena with whips and red-hot branding irons, defeated by his gladiatorial adversary and awaiting the judgement of the howling mob of spectators, who, together with the presiding official, held his fate in their fickle hands.

The gladiators, whose battles entertained the Roman people throughout the Republic and Empire, are among the most famous, and yet mysterious, groups in history. Their fame has been preserved in both the written and visual arts that have passed down to us through the centuries, and their exploits have inspired many films. From the classic *Spartacus* to the latest revival of the cinematic epic, *Gladiator*, these fearsome fighting men (and women) continue to grip our imaginations.

The life of a Roman gladiator was filled with excitement and danger. They were among the toughest of warriors, their harsh training preparing them for the titanic battles they would wage against each other. It is a telling irony that although we know a great deal about the lives of gladiators as a group, we know very little about the lives of individuals. Needless to say, none left any records written from their point of view. The other reason for the lack of information is simple enough: very few of them lived long enough to become famous even in their own time. Most gladiators could reasonably expect to fight only two or three times before being killed in the arena. With the exception of Spartacus, none really earned a significant place in recorded history. Although we know the names of some gladiators, and can point to various passages in classical literature describing their exploits, we have virtually no in-depth knowledge of their individual lives.

Life as a gladiator in ancient Rome was an abyss of bloody darkness illuminated only faintly by the prospect of honour, wealth, public adulation and the amorous attentions of adoring women. Most were drawn from the disinherited ranks of criminals, slaves and prisoners of war. Only very few free citizens chose to join the ranks of the gladiators. The odds on surviving, let alone prospering, were incredibly slight.

The first gladiatorial contest at Rome itself took place in 264 BC, and was staged by Decimus Junius Brutus in honour of his deceased father. The bloody contest was between three pairs of slaves, known as *bustuarii* (from *bustum*, meaning tomb or funeral pyre), and was held in the *forum boarium*, a commercial market area. This contest was called a *munus*, or 'duty' paid to a dead ancestor by his descendants, with the intention of keeping alive his memory. It is likely that the contests began on the ninth day after the funeral, which marked the end of the period of mourning.

In the years following the *munus* of Decimus Junius Brutus, further *munera* were held for distinguished persons. These would be repeated at five yearly intervals after the person's death or, in some cases, every year. According to the second-century AD scholar Festus, gladiatorial combat functioned as a less cruel substitute for the human sacrifice that had previously been practised. These sacrifices had served the purpose of nourishing the dead with the blood of the living, a phenomenon observed in many ancient cultures. Modern scholars agree with Festus, pointing out that gladiatorial contests were somewhat of an improvement over human sacrifice, since at least the winner came out of the ritual alive, and sometimes the loser also.

The practice of using the *forum boarium* for the contests quickly became established. Previously, this area had been the site of butchers' and market-gardeners' stalls, but these were later replaced by smarter trades, who decorated their facades with shields captured from the local enemies of Rome. It was a vibrant, bustling area, filled with people jostling each other in the heat and noise. The roughly rectangular central area of the *forum boarium*, which was bounded on the south-east by the *Circus Maximus* (home of the great chariot races) and by the Tiber on the west, contained two ranks of shops on one side, and on the other the temple of Concord. It also contained the twin temples of Fortuna and Mater Matuta, which had been built at the end of the sixth century BC, and their altars. A number of monuments, such as the temple to Portunus (the god of ports) and the circular temple to Hercules, would later be built here.

The early gladiatorial battles were rather basic, primitive affairs, without the extravagance and refinement in cruelty that would be witnessed later in the amphitheatres at Rome and other cities and towns. Indeed, in their original form, they were watched by very few spectators, who had to squeeze in against each other, pushing and jostling, straining and craning their necks to get a look at the bloody action being played out before them. These rough congregations, in which the spectators quickly planted themselves wherever they could find a place with a decent view, contained the seeds of the great spectacles of later years. They were primitive showcases for fighting and nothing more, and were certainly not prepared or stage-managed in the manner that would later become commonplace. At this stage, the *munera* were still viewed exclusively in terms of religious ceremony, this feeling perhaps enhanced by the very close quarters at which the battles were experienced. Women were not allowed to attend.

It was not long, however, before seats were added and hired out to the spectators, who were thus afforded a little more comfort as they watched each pair of gladiators fight. At this stage, they were all armed in the same manner: that of the Samnites, a fierce mountain people of southern Italy conquered by Rome in the fourth century BC. Each gladiator would carry a long, rectangular shield (*scutum*), a straight sword (*gladius*, from which the word 'gladiator' derives), a helmet and greaves (leg armour). Although we do not know exactly how these combats were organised, it is clear that the number of pairs taking part increased steadily throughout the first century of gladiatorial *munera*, from three to twenty-five to sixty. But the fact that the numbers of gladiators taking part in combats rose does not mean that the combats themselves were common at this time. They were, in fact, still exceptional.

The origin of the ceremonies themselves was shrouded in mystery even to the Romans themselves, although it is likely that the *munera*, as duties paid to the dead, or more precisely, rituals performed in recollection of sacred funerary ceremonies, emerged from the practice of sacrificing slaves or prisoners of war in memory of the illustrious dead. Legend has it that this originated in Campania (which would later become a great centre of gladiatorial training), at the behest of ancient gods, some of whom were said still to live in various places around the Mediterranean. Like all legends, this has to be treated with caution: many of the early texts supporting this thesis were produced by Christian propagandists seeking to discredit paganism.

According to the historian Festus: 'It was the custom to sacrifice prisoners on the tombs of valorous warriors; when the cruelty of this custom became evident, it was decided to make gladiators fight before the tomb.' If the manner of the deaths of these unfortunates was somewhat altered, the purpose remained the same: their blood was spilled to appease the spirits of the dead. The Romans, who imported ideas of the afterlife from Greece and Etruria, feared and respected the powers of the dead, as did many ancient peoples. They believed that on occasions they could gain entry to the realm of the living and perform all manner of mischief, including dragging people back with them to the other world. These fears were to a large degree put to rest by various public and private ceremonies aimed at limiting the powers of the dead, and confining their return to Earth to certain days.

Although the dead were feared and respected, in the religion of ancient Rome they were not seen as inherently dangerous and aggressive. Their hostility was only aroused if the duties to them were not performed in the proper way. A dead man was seen by the Romans as a shadow emptied of its substance, a 'lack'. It was with the spilling of human blood, the very fluid of life itself, that the dead were given back a transitory reality, and thus propitiated.

However, as the years passed, the connection with religious rites began to fade until the gladiatorial combats were attended for their own sake. The *munera* were infrequent in comparison to the other *ludi* (games), such as the chariot races, and this must account in great measure for their enormous popularity. Their importance to the political life of Rome also grew considerably, particularly during the Republic, when the Senate maintained a tight control over all forms of public spectacle, with the exception of gladiatorial combats. All other events were fixed within a calendar of spectacles, controlled by the magistrates.

THE CALENDAR OF SPECTACLES

Like many ancient peoples, the Romans celebrated the cycle of nature with a series of festivals, in which the gods on whom the harvest depended were appeased for another year. During the course of Rome's growth and military victories, these were in many cases appropriated as civic celebrations, although links with gods was maintained. Eventually, they were a regular event during the entire year, and became an important part of the rhythm of Roman life.

In the spring, from 28 April to 3 May, the *Ludi Florales* were held to ensure a good harvest. The audience, dressed in multi-coloured garments evoking nature's patchwork of colours, was treated to theatrical performances and circus games, which included letting loose hares and goats, symbolising fertility. The proceedings were then rounded off with a sacrifice to the goddess Flora. All kinds of people came to these *ludi*, including commoners and prostitutes (the prostitutes came to regard it as their feast), and as night fell, celebrations of a more carnal nature spread through the heaving crowds. The festival was suffused with drink and desire, and even the actresses in the theatrical presentations threw off their clothes when the audience demanded it.

Not all the games were a yearly event. The *Ludi Saeculares* were celebrated every century in May and June, and were intended to ensure the continuation of the world for another hundred years. They took place at night in the *Campus Martius*, and were originally founded (according to legend) by Publius Valerius Poplicola in 509 BC. One of his ancestors, it was said, had discovered, twenty feet underground, the altar of the under-world deities Dis Pater and Proserpina.

The gods of the underworld (Dis Inferi) were said to be responsible for outbreaks of plague, which were seen as manifestations of their displeasure. It was important to appease them, and this was the reason for the *Ludi Taurei Quinquennales*, held every five years on 25 and 26 June. During these *ludi*, games were held in the *Circus Flaminius,* including horse racing, bull fighting and sacrifice. Their last recorded celebration was in 186 BC.

The *Ludi Apollinares* were celebrated for the first time in 211 BC in honour of Apollo, whose help had been sought against Hannibal. Rome had recently been heavily defeated by the Carthaginian invader and the city had seemed doomed. Eventually, however, Hannibal was driven from Italy and Rome controlled the eastern Mediterranean. Every year thereafter Apollo's games were held from 6 to 13 July, including theatrical presentations and hunts of wild animals. Apollo was also regarded as a healing god, and was worshipped during the games with sacrifices, during which all present wore garlands.

At the end of July, as the crops ripened in the fields, another set of games would be held called the *Ludi Victoriae Caesaris*, in honour of Julius Caesar and of the goddess Victoria, who was closely connected with Caesar. These games were established after the battle of Pharsalus in 48 BC, and consisted of circus games and scenic events.

Other events on the calendar have a less certain origin, and several lost their original focus quite quickly. The *Ludi Romani* were originally celebrated on 13 September in honour of a triumph and dedicated to Jupiter Optimus Maximus. According to Livy, they became permanent in 366 BC. But later they came to be held between 4 and 19 September. They began with a procession from the Capitol to the *Circus Maximus*, where a sacrifice was made.

Little is known of the *Ludi Capitolini*, which were held on 15 October in honour of Jupiter. They were not public games, but were given by the priests of Jupiter Capitolinus in Rome. It is possible that the games were held in celebration of the conquest of Veii in Italy, or perhaps the saving of the Capitol from the Gauls.

As winter drew in, the games continued. The *Ludi Victoriae Sullanae* were held from 26 October to 1 November in honour of the goddess Victoria. Established in 81 BC to celebrate Sulla's victory on 1 November 82 BC over the Samnites at the *Porta Collina* in Rome, they included circus games on the anniversary of the battle.

Starting very soon after on 4 November, and running for two weeks, the *Ludi Plebeii* were second only to the *Ludi Romani* in importance. Probably established in 220 BC by Gaius Flaminius, they were held in honour of Jupiter. An alternative theory of their origin is that they were created by the plebeians themselves after they had been deprived of an age-old wine festival which they had celebrated in September.

THE MUNERA

Against this backdrop of civic and religious festivals, the *munera* were originally different, at one step removed from the city's leadership as, until 105 BC they were only given by individuals, although they were included among the official events. Although in principle anyone could organise and put on a *munus*, the enormous cost of staging them, which usually included a gigantic banquet for the spectators afterwards, ensured that only the very wealthy actually did so. At such banquets, only the finest and most exotic dishes would be served. The first course might consist of lettuce (which was considered a good aid to digestion) and leeks, followed by pickled tuna garnished with eggs. The first course would be rounded off with more eggs, cheese and olives. The next course consisted of a huge variety of dishes, including sow's udder, wild fowl, barnyard hens, boar, antelope, hare, gazelle and even flamingo. The guests at such a banquet would eat without cutlery, and slaves would occasionally be called upon to wipe their hands. While most banquets would be attended with some politeness, it was not unusual to see the famous Roman habit of vomiting in order to prolong the pleasure of eating. It was also considered wise to follow the dictates of nature, and so the guests happily belched and farted and even urinated into a chamber pot held by a slave while still at the table.

One such banquet is vividly described by the Roman poet and satirist Juvenal (c. AD 60–c. 140). Juvenal had known poverty when he fell out of favour with the Emperor Domitian and was exiled penniless to Eygpt. Although he later found a patron in the Emperor Hadrian and was free to write his great satires, he never lost his profound sympathy for the poor. This is often best expressed by his disgust for the obscene extravagances of the rich. An after-games banquet gives him all the material he needs: amid the braying din and piled-up food, he notices a woman who 'souses the floor with the washings of her insides . . . she drinks and vomits like a big snake that has tumbled into a vat.'

But such was the popularity of the *munera* that few politicians with deep pockets could resist the chance to be associated with staging one. They soon became an excellent means by which those with political aspirations could gain favour with the populace and thus increase their prospects in elections.

In the first century BC, the format of the *munera* was altered considerably, and while the idea of a duty paid to the dead was ostensibly maintained, in fact gladiatorial combats were given on the flimsiest of pretexts. The plebeians, who originally considered the games to be a privilege bestowed upon them by the wealthy and powerful, now began to see them as a right. At the same time, as more and more *munera* were staged, greater and more unusual splendours were demanded by the audiences. It was around this time that the *venatio*, or wild-beast hunt, was added to the *munus*. At first an occasional treat, under the Empire it became the accepted accompaniment to the *munus*. Always keen to make an impact, the stagers of the games tried out all sorts of gimmicks. Julius Caesar (c. 100–44 BC) had his gladiators dressed in silver armour, an idea that was immediately taken up by several other noblemen – and immediately went out of fashion.

Whatever the success of the latest innovations, gladiatorial games remained hugely popular with the people of Rome. It was not uncommon, for example, for people in a town where a prominent citizen, such as a lawyer or politician, had died to demand a promise from his survivors that a combat would be held in his honour. Such was the mania for the games that later Emperors had to place a limit on how much could be spent on staging such contests to save members of the elite from bankrupting themselves to win favour with the people. The senatorial decree of the Emperor Marcus Aurelius, in AD 176, divided gladiatorial games into five categories: under 30,000 sesterces; 30 to 60,000; 60 to 100,000; 100 to 150,000; and 150 to 200,000 sesterces, which was the maximum. The prices of gladiators too were divided into bands, ranging from 1,000 to 15,000 sesterces.

The staging of gladiatorial contests spread with the empire itself, and evidence of them had been found throughout the imperial territories. The popularity of the games in Rome meant that their presence further afield was seen as an important method of Romanising conquered lands. Since Roman soldiers enjoyed watching gladiatorial contests, they would be staged for them in whatever new region they were occupying.

To the people of ancient Rome the arena of gladiatorial combat was a reflection of the awesome strength, power and indeed civilisation of their mighty empire, whose territorial achievements had been secured through military violence. Rome was a martial society, strong and powerful, whose wealth had been secured through military conquest, and so it placed great emphasis on personal courage and physical endurance. To the people of Rome, how one faced death was at least as important as how one lived one's life. A gladiator was taught to kill – and to die – well. He was taught exactly how to take the life of his opponent, with a swift sword thrust to the neck, and to be utterly unmoved by the thick gouts of blood that would follow from the *coup de grace*. He was taught how to receive the death blow when he had been defeated and the spectators were in no mood to show clemency, without cringing or shrinking back from the sword, without crying out as the blade entered his flesh and his life blood cascaded on to the hot sand of the arena.

As in most ancient societies, life expectancy in Rome was not high, and the vast majority could not reasonably expect to live far beyond the age of thirty. It was thus extremely important to meet one's death with courage, honour and dignity – indeed, to look on death with contempt; a Roman citizen had only to visit the arena to witness these qualities in awesome abundance. In the militaristic culture of ancient Rome, prowess in hand-to-hand combat, the art of killing, was viewed with a respect that originated in the glory of triumph and the conquest of other peoples; and it was the ability to kill an enemy single-handedly upon which Rome depended for the maintenance of its empire.

The idea of gladiatorial combat was thus perfectly natural to the people of ancient Rome, and the spectacles inspired excitement and the enjoyment of battles well fought, rather than horror and disgust. Indeed, many elements of gladiatorial combat have found their way down the centuries to the modern world, not least of which is the behaviour of the spectators to such events. There is a certain grim humour to be found in the descriptions of these supporters, in the uncomfortable recognition we experience in reading of them. One contemporary observer of the games was the great historian and senator Publius Cornelius Tacitus (AD 56 – after 117). Of impeccable patrician credentials, Tacitus held the offices of quaestor in 79, praetor in 88 and consul in 97. His early works display expertise in a wide range of fields, including education, biography and ethnography and in his later years he wrote two great histories of Rome. In one, he describes some rather unfortunate events that attended the staging of a gladiatorial spectacle in Pompeii in AD 59:

> There was a serious riot between the people of Pompeii and Nuceria, a nearby town. It arose out of a trifling incident at a gladiatorial show given by a man who had been expelled from the Roman senate [the reason is unknown, but it may have been immorality of some kind], Livineius Regulus. During an exchange of taunts – characteristic of these disorderly country towns – abuse led to stone-throwing, and then swords were drawn. The people of Pompeii, where the show was held, came off best. Many wounded and mutilated Nucerians were taken to the capital. Many bereavements, too, were suffered by parents and children.

Most gladiators came from the lowest ranks of Roman society, and were considered in that light by the people. If a criminal, or a disobedient slave or a prisoner of war was lucky – or unlucky – enough to possess a strong body and resourceful mind, he might well find himself recruited, whether he liked it or not, into a *familia gladiatoria* (a gladiatorial troupe). Surprisingly, their ranks were swelled, also, by some free-born men who had decided, quite voluntarily, to give up their citizen rights and bind themselves body and soul to the owner of the troupe, the *lanista*.

The senator and author Petronius (c. AD 27–66) had much to say on the recruitment of gladiators. His full name was probably Gaius (or Titus) Petronius Niger, and he was referred to as *Arbiter Elegantiae* ('judge of elegance') by Tacitus. Because of his profound sense of luxury and elegance, he was responsible for many of the entertainments at Nero's court. He was also the author of the *Satyricon*, an often bawdy description of life in the first century AD, and the earliest known example in Europe of the picaresque novel. Such was Petronius' influence on Nero that it aroused the jealousy of the politician Gaius Ofonius Tigellinus (d. 69 AD), who brought a number of false accusations against him. Petronius knew that Nero's anger would result in his death, and so he committed suicide, after writing a lengthy description of Nero's vices and sending it to him in a final stylistic flourish. According to Petronius, newly recruited gladiators swore an oath 'to endure branding, chains, flogging or death by the sword', to follow their master's orders without question and to pay for the food and drink they received with their blood. Once this oath had been taken, the free man lost his *libertas* and became a slave, the property of the lanista. These were surely among the harshest terms of any profession; nevertheless, it has been estimated that by the end of the Republic (55–31 BC), about half of all gladiators were volunteers.

Why would free men choose such a course, exchanging liberty and the rights of the Roman citizen for whips, chains and the extreme likelihood of a violent and agonising death? What dreadful events in an otherwise presumably orderly life could have forced them to decide that there really was no alternative to becoming a gladiator, with all the suffering (inflicted by them and upon them) that this profession would entail? Could it have been the desire for danger and adventure? The need for money? Perhaps it was a profound and desperate need for the glow of public adulation to brighten an otherwise undistinguished life, to give it meaning, even if the language of that meaning was suffused with suffering and death.

Unlikely as it may seem, there were numerous advantages to the profession of gladiator. For one thing, they were renowned throughout the Republic for their courage, morale and absolute loyalty to their master. The martial discipline they maintained also meant that they received a level of respect and honour otherwise reserved for the Roman army itself.

For some citizens, the choice to enrol in a gladiatorial school was made purely as a result of economic factors: some were aristocrats who had squandered their inherited wealth and found themselves without the means to make a decent living. As gladiators, they would get three square meals a day, good medical care and the opportunity to win money and goods in addition to their payment for appearing in the arena. If they managed to survive long enough, they would eventually be granted their freedom. In addition to those high up the social scale who had fallen on hard times, there were many economically marginal citizens who did not have a trade, and whose career options were limited to the army, teaching, a life of crime and the gladiatorial schools. To these types, life as a gladiator would not have been such an unattractive option, especially since gladiators did not fight more than two or three times a year. If they managed to avoid a bloody and painful death, they had a chance of fame and wealth, not to mention rewards of a more carnal nature, as these examples of graffiti from Pompeii illustrate:

Celadus the Thracian, three times victor and three times crowned, adored by young girls.

Crescens the nocturnal netter [*retiarius*] of young girls.

Thrax is the heart-throb of all the girls.

Gladiators were not only 'adored by young girls'. They were also the objects of the amorous attentions of wealthy aristocratic women. It is easy enough to imagine how such infatuations could develop. For a woman possessing a high rank in society, unused to the trials and vicissitudes to which the masses were subjected, boredom must have been a more or less constant companion. At the games could be found all the excitement and carnage she could possibly wish for, as the gladiators, their muscular bodies sweating and blood-stained, stalked each other across the arena. Indeed, it was perhaps the sight of the scars themselves that plunged such women into the depths of ecstasy.

It must have been a heady brew – the bloody wounds, the flexing muscles, the violent death – and a forbidden one, for the gladiators were considered to be no better than prostitutes. To commit adultery was bad enough; but to commit adultery with a gladiator must have enhanced the illicit passion of these women a hundredfold.

One such affair which achieved great notoriety is described by the poet and satirist Juvenal, who gives full vent to his indignation in describing the indiscretions of a senator's wife named Eppia, who eloped to Egypt with her gladiator lover.

EPPIA'S PASSION

The story of Eppia illustrates the level of passion the gladiators inspired in women, many of whom occupied the highest levels of Roman society. As the historian Roland Auguet notes in his *Cruelty and Civilisation: The Roman Games* (1972), 'those who gave way to it were not modest young girls naively moved by the prestige of a helmet, but mature and wealthy matrons'. Juvenal himself is at pains to remind us that Eppia was the wife of a senator, and that her childhood was spent surrounded by every luxury her father's wealth could provide: she slept 'on swansdown, in a cradle trimmed with gold'.

The battle-hardened gladiator with whom Eppia fell in love was named Sergiolus and, contrary to what we might expect, he seems not to have been blessed with good looks. In fact, he was getting on in years, and his beard was turning grey, which prompted him to shave it. His nose was deformed by a large bump, caused by many years of wearing a helmet, and an 'acrid humour' dripped constantly from one of his eyes. The picture we have of Sergiolus, therefore, is not a particularly salubrious one: he seems to have been a man about whom clung a penumbra of blood, death and sorrow. Juvenal takes the opportunity to provide a sardonic portrait of this ineligible bachelor:

What was the youthful charm that Eppia found so
   enchanting?
What did she see worth while being labelled 'The
   Gladiatress'?
This dear boy had begun to shave a long while ago, and one
   arm,
Wounded, gave hope of retirement; besides, he was
   frightfully ugly,
Scarred by his helmet, a wart on his nose, and his eyes always
   running.
Gladiators, though, look better than any Adonis:
This is what she preferred to children, country, and sister,
This to her husband. The sword is what they dote on, these
   women.

In spite of everything, this was a man for whom Eppia was
prepared to endure the full opprobrium and condemnation of
Roman society. Her passionate love for Sergiolus ensured that
Eppia suffered other discomforts also. The *familia gladiatoria* to
which Sergiolus belonged travelled widely among the provinces,
going as far afield as Asia Minor and Egypt, and Eppia must have
found herself making many long journeys in less than comfortable conditions. Juvenal makes a typically wry comment on
these travels:

> To go aboard ship is torture under a husband's orders: then
> the smell of the bilges is sickening, then the sky wheels
> dizzily around. But a wife who's off with her lover suffers no
> qualms. The one vomits over her husband, the other sits down
> to a hearty meal with the crew, takes a turn on the quarter-
> deck, helps haul on the sheets, and enjoys it.

This must have been the case with Eppia, as she strode upon the
heaving deck of the ship, and watched the gleaming façades of

her beloved Rome gradually dwindle in the distance. In terms of her place in society, and the regard in which she was held by her peers, Eppia made a considerable sacrifice – perhaps the ultimate one for a woman so privileged. This is amply demonstrated by the nickname by which she was subsequently called: 'Gladiatrix', or female gladiator. This was a serious insult, as gladiators had less social status than even a slave. This view is reinforced by the erroneous insistence of Latin authors that the gladiators' food was vile and disgusting; in fact, it was of the same quality as that of soldiers. Nevertheless, the food the gladiators ate was considered as a metaphor for the foulness and misery inherent in their profession, 'the price paid for the purchase of marketable blood'. It seems incredible that Eppia should have given up her privileged life in the upper echelons of society, leaving behind her husband and children forever, for Sergiolus and his violent, bestial world. But this is precisely what she did, for Sergiolus was a gladiator.

Of course Eppia's case was undoubtedly an extreme one, and the erotic attraction felt by many women towards their favourite gladiators usually led to more subtle indiscretions, such as spending a couple of hours every day at the *ludus* (gladiators' barracks), taking up the gladiators' weapons and attacking the *palus*, the wooden stake used in training for combat.

THE CONCEPTION OF COMMODUS

Occasionally, the amorous feelings inspired by the sight of a gladiator could have extremely unfortunate repercussions for the gladiator himself, as we can see from this passage from Juvenal:

Faustina, daughter of Antoninus Pius and wife of Marcus Aurelius, having seen the gladiators pass one day, conceived the most violent love for one of them; and this passion having

ఌ 25 ഔ

made her ill for a long time, she confessed it to her husband. Chaldeans whom Marcus Aurelius consulted said that it was necessary that this gladiator should be killed and that Faustina should bathe in his blood and afterwards lie with her husband. When this advice had been followed, the empress' passion was in fact spent, but she brought into the world Commodus, who was more of a gladiator than a prince.

The hero of the tale is the hapless gladiator, who had the misfortune to excite the passion of an empress who had happened to see him walk past in a parade. The events which follow have the piquant flavour of some strange epic of the supernatural, charged with dark eroticism. The debilitating passion of Faustina; the act of confession to her husband, in which she admits to her terrible sexual obsession; Marcus Aurelius' desperate recourse to supernatural aid; the dreadful solution in which the gladiator is murdered; his blood staining her body as Faustina makes love with her husband; the connection between sex and human sacrifice and the birth of the awful Commodus, bringer of torture and death to so many . . . All these elements revolve around an initial event which might seem simple enough, but which in fact signified a deep and terrible iniquity: the act of falling in love with a gladiator.

Love affairs between participants in the games and nobles were not always heterosexual in nature. The politician and historian Dio Cassius (c. AD 150–235), who held office under the Emperors Commodus, Pertinax, Septimius Severus and Alexander Severus, and who held the consulship in 220 and 229, provides a description of the circumstances in which the Emperor Elagabalus (third century AD) fell in love with the charioteer Hierocles.

Hierocles, during the games in the circus, fell from his chariot directly in front of the seat of Elagabalus. As he fell, his helmet came off. Noticed by the prince – he had a beardless chin and long, fair hair – he was immediately picked up and taken to the palace.

THE SCANDAL OF THE FEMALE GLADIATORS

It is from the great biographer and historian Suetonius that we read of the strange practice of using female gladiators in the arena. Born in Rome to a military tribune, he counted Pliny the Younger among his friends and Pliny was also his patron, recommending him to the Emperor Trajan, who gave him a military tribunate (a tribune was an official chosen by the plebeians to protect their rights against the patricians). A later patron, Septicius Clarus, helped Suetonius to secure the position of keeper of the archives. This position, together with that of secretary to the Emperor Hadrian, enabled Suetonius to examine the documents that were useful in writing his *Lives of the Caesars* (c. AD 121), which covers the Emperors from Julius Caesar to Domitian. According to Suetonius:

> Domitian presented many extravagant entertainments in the Colosseum and the Circus. Besides the usual two-horse chariot races he staged a couple of battles, one for infantry, the other for cavalry; a sea-fight in the amphitheatre; wild-beast hunts; gladiatorial shows by torchlight in which women as well as men took part . . .

The crucial ingredient was novelty; Domitian also enjoyed watching female gladiators fight with dwarves. These more unusual battles were also extremely popular with the Roman citizenry. It is a pity that more information on these fighters has not survived, although there are visual representations, such as a relief from Halicarnassus in the eastern Aegean showing two female gladiators fighting. There are also inscriptions mentioning two names: Achillia and Amazon. Classical authors also mention them, for instance Petronius describes a gladiatress who fought from a British-style chariot.

If it was considered disgraceful for a man of high social standing to enrol as a gladiator, for a noblewoman to do so was utterly beyond the pale. Juvenal was especially outraged by their unseemly antics:

How can a woman be decent
Sticking her head in a helmet, denying the sex she was born with?
Manly feats they adore, but they wouldn't want to be men,
Poor weak things (they think), how little they really enjoy it!
What a great honour it is for a husband to see, at an auction
Where his wife's effects are up for sale, belts, shin-guards,
Arm-protectors and plumes!
Hear her grunt and groan as she works at it, parrying, thrusting;
See her neck bent down under the weight of her helmet . . .
Ah, degenerate girls from the line of our praetors and consuls,
Tell us, whom have you seen got up in any such fashion,
Panting and sweating like this? No gladiator's wench,
No tough strip-tease broad would ever so much as attempt it.

The presence of female gladiators in the arena steadily increased over the years, particularly during the reign of Nero in the first century AD. However, the practice was specifically outlawed by the Emperor Septimus Severus in the early third century AD, perhaps because the numbers of women performing had become alarming.

To the minds of intellectuals like Juvenal, the practice of placing women in the arena to fight as gladiators was another source for the ridicule which he heaped upon Roman society; and yet the presence of women in these places of blood and death suggests, curiously enough, a certain equality in the context of the particular *virtus* (or skill) of killing and facing death with courage and dignity. It seems that in ancient Rome, this *virtus* was considered of greater importance than gender.

LEAN TIMES

In times of famine or other shortages, gladiators were among those who were considered to be owed nothing by the state, and so were unceremoniously kicked out of Rome. Suetonius has this to say, regarding the grain crisis of AD 6 –7:

> Augustus showed . . . dignity and strength of character on another occasion when, after announcing a distribution of largesse, he found that the list of citizens had been swelled by a considerable number of recently freed slaves. He gave out that those to whom he had promised nothing were entitled to nothing, and that he refused to increase the total sum; thus the original beneficiaries must be content with less. In one period of exceptional scarcity he found it impossible to cope with the public distress except by expelling every useless mouth from the city, such as the slaves in the slave-market, all members of the gladiatorial schools, all foreign residents with the exception of physicians and teachers, and a number of household-slaves.

The phrase 'every useless mouth' reveals the true light in which gladiators were seen in the Roman state, regardless of the adulation they received from the population when times were good. They were truly the lowest of the low, no more than commodities to be dumped when economic factors made them unacceptably expensive.

CHAPTER TWO

A Branch of
Politics

II

As might be expected of a pursuit that was so fantastically popular, the gladiatorial games had a great political significance. During the Roman Republic, whoever gave the most impressive contest gained great popularity with the people, and could expect to do particularly well at election time. In fact, the growth of gladiatorial contests was the result of fierce rivalry, intrigue and political competition among aristocrats, who continually jostled each other for power. One of the most striking examples of these competitions, and the political manoeuvrings to which they gave rise, is the *munus* put on by Julius Caesar in 65 BC.

Gaius Julius Caesar, who laid the foundations of the Roman Imperial system, was born in 100 BC, and belonged to the illustrious Julian clan. Political controversy surrounded him even at an early age, chiefly as a result of the struggle between the *Populares* (led by Gaius Marius, Caesar's uncle by marriage), a party supporting agrarian reform, and the *Optimates*, an aristocratic, reactionary senatorial group. In 84 BC, Caesar married Cornelia, the daughter of Marius's associate Cinna. When Marius's enemy and leader of the *Optimates*, Lucius Cornelius Sulla (138–78 BC), became dictator in 82 BC, Caesar's marriage marked him as a potential target for assassination. However, he was merely ordered to divorce Cornelia. This he refused to do and instead left Rome, and did not return until 78 BC, after Sulla's resignation.

He was unable to gain office, and so left Rome once again to study rhetoric in Rhodes, before returning in 73 BC. Caesar put on a *munus* in 65 BC, the year of his aedileship (an *aedile* was an elected official who was responsible for public works, games, the supervision of markets and the grain and water supplies). According to Suetonius, he planned to:

> put on a gladiatorial show, but had collected so immense a troop of combatants that his terrified political opponents rushed a bill through the House, limiting the number that anyone might keep in Rome; consequently far fewer pairs fought than had been advertised.

This spectacle was ostensibly in memory of Caesar's father, but it is undeniable that the aim was also to win political favour for his candidacy for the praetorship. This was the reason his enemies acted against him, forcing him to make do with considerably fewer gladiators for his *munus*. Nevertheless, the number of pairs of gladiators he was able to present still amounted to 320, resulting in a fine performance.

Suetonius describes Caesar's gladiatorial shows in some detail:

> His public shows were of great variety. They included a gladiatorial contest, stage-plays for every Roman ward performed in several languages, chariot-races in the Circus, athletic competitions, and a mock naval battle. At the gladiatorial contest in the Forum, a man named Furius Leptinus, of praetorian family, fought Quintus Calpenus, a barrister and former senator, to the death . . .
>
> Wild-beast hunts took place five days running, and the entertainment ended with a battle between two armies, each consisting of 500 infantry, twenty elephants, and thirty cavalry. To let the camps be pitched facing each other, Caesar

removed the central barrier of the Circus, around which the chariots ran . . .

The naval battle was fought on an artificial lake dug in the Lesser Codeta, between Tyrian and Egyptian ships, with two, three, or four banks of oars, and heavily manned. Such huge numbers of visitors flocked to these shows from all directions that many of them had to sleep in tents pitched along the streets or roads, or on roof tops; and often the pressure of the crowd crushed people to death. The victims included two senators.

THE PERIL OF A LOUD VOICE

In the Roman Empire, not only elections but also sponsorship of the games was largely taken out of the hands of the citizenry. After all, the Emperor did not want sundry prominent citizens gaining popular favour by putting on splendid battles. As a tool of political propaganda, the games were of very great importance, and the Emperors were quick to turn them to their own advantage. The Emperor thus became the regular sponsor of the games in Rome (with the exception of those held in December), deciding on their scope, duration and date, usually holding them on important occasions such as anniversaries and victories. He would also regularly attend them, allowing them to take on an additional political meaning. Although they could not vote, the people were afforded an opportunity to communicate directly with their Emperor at a *munus*. Safety in numbers and the anonymity of a large crowd meant that at times they expressed their feelings quite loudly and forthrightly, and on occasion even criticised the Emperor himself. Of course, the same anonymity that allowed each individual to avoid a very unwise direct confrontation with the Emperor also detracted from the impact of his grievance. And so the symbol of direct communication with the ruler was of greater significance than what was actually said, and the likelihood of the Emperor acting upon it.

Nevertheless, there were occasions when shouting too loudly could put a person in considerable peril. The fate of the Emperor himself could, however, be directly influenced by his reaction to the crowd at a *munus*. When Caligula (AD 12–41) refused to listen to the grievances of the crowd, and attempted to have soldiers execute the most vocal members, the crowd was further infuriated, and the conspirators against him were emboldened to assassinate him. In showing himself as sympathetic to the crowd, however, a wise Emperor could profit politically. A demonstration that the government was not impersonal and impervious to public opinion could do wonders for an Emperor's public relations, and showing himself to be a fellow spectator not averse to rubbing shoulders, so to speak, with the masses, was an easy way of achieving this.

THE TWO-EDGED SWORD OF THE EMPEROR'S KINDNESS

While other individuals with the financial means were not actually forbidden from giving *munera*, it would not have been a particularly good idea for them to do so. Any magistrate, for instance, who took the decision to spend a significant portion of his fortune on staging a *munus*, thus exciting the admiration of the people, would almost certainly have been considered a potential threat by an Emperor, whose jealousy was quick to flare up. The result could be exile, or worse. The person giving the *munus* could quite easily end up as a participant in one. This was not the case, however, in provinces such as Thrace, Macedonia, Aquitania and Mauretania, where magistrates were free to flatter the vanity of the people with spectacular *munera*, without fear of offending a far-off Emperor. In the provinces the Emperor's representatives used the games to offer up praise not to the dead, but to their distant leader, around whom all the religious and emotional feelings aroused by the spectacles would crystallize.

In Rome it was extremely important to hold *munera* as frequently as possible, such was the level of their popularity amongst the plebeians. To allow too long a period to pass without a spectacle would be to court unpopularity, which brought with it inevitable danger. This inspired the Emperor on some occasions to renounce the privilege in favour of the magistrates. There was a very good reason for this: when the privilege of staging a *munus* was bestowed upon a magistrate, he had no choice but to meet the responsibility – the consequences of failing in this of all duties were unthinkable. This happened particularly in December, the month in which officials were allowed to stage combats rather than the Emperor. However, there were strict limits on the number of gladiators who could fight (these restrictions were not, of course, imposed upon the Emperor). Thus, the *munera* given by magistrates could not hope to compare with those given by the Emperor, and their value as entertainment – and thus propaganda – was considerably reduced. The advantage to the Emperor in this was threefold: the plebeians were given their spectacle, its costs were borne by the magistrates obliged to stage it, and those who might have harboured ambitions against the Emperor were subtly prevented from gaining too much public favour.

The orator Fronto in his *Letters* describes the political importance of staging exciting gladiatorial spectacles while discussing the rule of the wise Emperor Trajan. Born in Italica, near Seville, Spain, to a family of probable Roman origin, Trajan was Emperor from 98 to 117. As a youth he undertook military training, and served in the Roman army in Spain, Syria and Germany during the reigns of Titus and Domitian. He was a highly successful general, and in 91 was elected as a consul. The Emperor Nerva adopted him in 97, and upon Nerva's death the following year, Trajan became Emperor.

Although he did not return to Rome for several years, he immediately distinguished himself as a good Emperor by donating money to his soldiers and ensuring the wellbeing of the children of poor freemen in Rome and other cities in Italy. In 101, Trajan began his first campaign against Dacia (which occupied present-day west-central Romania). The country took five years to subdue, and the conquest was celebrated by four months of games, and the creation of the famous column in Trajan's Forum in Rome.

In 113, Trajan again left Rome, this time on a campaign against the Parthians. He captured the Parthian capital, Ctesiphon, on the River Tigris, and also annexed Armenia and northern Mesopotamia. In common with other Roman commanders, Trajan took inspiration from Alexander the Great, and at the end of his Parthian campaign, when he had reached the mouth of the River Euphrates, he is said to have wept, lamenting the fact that he could go no further and equal Alexander's accomplishments. There was a good deal of unrest in the newly acquired territories, not to mention the rest of the Empire, including tribal uprisings in Britain, a Jewish rebellion and ominous stirrings of unrest on the lower Danube.

In failing health, Trajan set sail for Italy, but died in 117 at Selinus in Cilicia (Turkey). His reign was distinguished by administrative reforms and a number of major construction projects, including roads, canals and bridges, the restoration of the Appian Way between Rome and Capua, and the draining of the Pontine Marshes.

Fronto states that the Roman people were concerned especially with two things: the grain supply and spectacles. Trajan's rule, he goes on, won approval 'as much because of games as because of serious things'. Serious things, he says, are neglected with greater loss, but games are neglected with greater resentment.

CRUELTY AND JUSTICE

No one in their right mind would advocate the staging of gladiatorial contests in the present day. The sight of men and women slaying each other in the artificial battlefield of a blood-spattered arena would certainly not be tolerated. An average Roman citizen, however, would have looked on such a reaction with amusement and contempt. When we look at the games within their ancient cultural context, we can see that attendance at the amphitheatre was an essential part of being a Roman, a member of a powerful warrior state. Indeed, it is interesting to note that the most dramatic increase in the games' popularity occurred during the first two centuries AD, when peace throughout the Empire provided little opportunity for real warfare. In the absence of real battles in other parts of the Empire, the people made do with artificial battles (although real enough for the participants), the transformation of war into a spectator sport.

The gladiatorial contest quickly came to symbolise Roman military might, a fact well demonstrated by the Romans' use of their defeated enemies' armour and fighting techniques in the arena. It was also a warning to all parts of the Empire not to think of challenging Rome, whose citizens watched bloody slaughter for entertainment.

The games were not supported unanimously in Rome, however: some objected to the use of extreme violence as entertainment, albeit on the grounds that its vulgarity appealed to the lower classes, and for that reason alone should be avoided by anyone with a half-decent mind. Christian writers, naturally enough, strongly objected to the bloodshed in the arena, although many Christians were eager spectators, sometimes going directly from church to the games.

In spite of the undoubted cruelty inherent in the games, there was an underlying principle of justice. The audience expected to be entertained by a good, professional performance, and if a gladiator fought bravely and well, he could reasonably expect to be allowed to leave the arena alive, even if his opponent defeated him. From the Roman point of view, fighting bravely and dying nobly were of enormous moral importance, and any gladiator who found favour with his audience in these terms could frequently count on their willingness to allow him to leave the arena (this was known as *missio*).

One such occasion of clemency during the reign of Claudius is described for us by the writer and rhetorician Pliny the Younger. Pliny's reputation rests upon his ten books of letters, which cover a wide range of subjects, including the eruption of Vesuvius, his villa at Laurentum, the Roman policy towards Christians, and what may be the first written report on a haunted house (the house was in Athens, and was rented by the Stoic philosopher Athenodorus, who claimed to have seen an apparition complete with rattling chains). In his *Panegyricus* he describes the action that led to the exemptions:

> We saw a spectacle then not enervating and dissolute, nor one to soften and break the spirits of men, but one which inspired them to noble wounds and contempt for death, because the love of glory and the desire for victory was seen in the bodies of even slaves and criminals.

Gladiatorial games were also held by Emperors to prepare the Romans for war. In the *Historia Augusta* of Maximus et Balbinus, we read: 'I accept as more truthful the tradition that Romans about to go to war ought to have seen battles and wounds and steel, and naked men contending against each other, that they might not fear armed men or shrink from wounds and blood.'

The blood, violence and cruelty of the games illustrate the moral qualities the Romans considered to be most valuable. They also helped to explain to them the reason for the power and dominance of Rome.

CHAPTER THREE

How to Kill,
How to Die

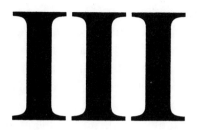

The Romans took their gladiators from several sources, most of them extremely unwilling. During the years of Imperial expansion, captured soldiers were an obvious and fruitful source, and even when the limits of the Empire had been established and secured, a rebellious province could still provide a handy source of malcontents with which to populate the arena. After they had subdued Judea, Titus and Vespasian seized vast numbers of Jews and condemned them to gladiatorial combat. Other prisoners were sold as slaves, thrown to the animals or otherwise massacred. The strongest, however, were usually sent to the gladiatorial schools (*ludi*).

Individuals convicted of serious criminal offences were also sentenced to gladiator schools; and disobedient or otherwise troublesome slaves were frequently sold to the notorious gladiatorial troupes by their owners, although under the Empire, laws were passed which required an owner to prove that the slave deserved such a fate. (Of course, they could also simply be condemned to public execution.)

FREEDOM FOR THE SWORD

Incredible as it may seem, alongside the criminals, slaves and prisoners of war who had no choice about becoming gladiators, there were, as we have seen, many free Roman citizens who, from the first years of the Empire, decided to throw in their lot with the *familia gladiatoria*. Once he had taken the dreadful oath to surrender his very life to the *lanista*, the free man was reduced to the status of a slave, a member of the *infames*, the pariahs, although he would regain his freedom if he survived long enough to complete his engagement. For these men, the degradation implicit in becoming a gladiator was outweighed by the excitement of the arena, not to mention the possibility, however remote, of success, fame and the wealth it would bring with it. In fact, if hard-up noblemen were looking for a tidy sum simply by enrolling as gladiators, they were disappointed: on enrolment they received at most 2,000 sesterces – not a great deal when one considers that a single banquet could cost three or four times that amount.

Once the oath had been taken, the new recruits were led into an extremely tough and depressing world. Once inside the *ludus*, they were taken to the cells lining the exercise square. One of the walls surrounding the square contained a huge kitchen, while elsewhere in the *ludus* was a dark, dank prison for recalcitrant gladiators. There was also an armoury, which contained the multiple instruments of death, the tools of the gladiator's dreadful trade. The oath they swore, to endure the whip, the branding iron and death by the sword implied no idle threat on the part of the *lanista*; these were indeed the punishments that difficult recruits could expect unless they followed their orders to the letter. And from the point of view of the *lanista*, these punishments were required to control the prisoners of war, the slaves and the criminals, to stamp out immediately any thoughts of rebellion. From the moment they entered the *ludus*, in fetters which prevented them even from standing up straight, the recruits were taught to expect nothing from their lives but pain, exhaustion, vicious punishments and the likelihood of a death agony endured amid the screams and howls of the crowded amphitheatre.

TRAINING OF THE KILLERS

The first steps of the training were overseen by the *doctores*, former gladiators whose expertise in the use of weapons had enabled them to survive the trials of the arena. Each *doctor* was expert in the use of a particular weapon and fighting technique, for example those of the Thracians, the Samnites and the Sagittarii, the latter using bows and arrows to bring their opponents down. In the centre of the rectangular yard stood the *palus*, the two-yard-high wooden stake upon which the gladiators practised their fighting technique. During these practices, they did not use proper weapons, but rather the *rudis*, a wooden sword. The *rudis* also served as the symbol of freedom which was presented to those gladiators who were skilful enough to be released from their service.

Elsewhere in the *ludus* there was an oval area exactly like the arena, a perfect replica in which the gladiators could practise their manoeuvres, perfecting the deadly skills they would need to prevail against their future opponents. When practising in this area, their wooden swords were cast aside in favour of real weapons, which were heavier than normal. The purpose of these heavier instruments was to build up the stamina they would need for the lengthy, energy-sapping battles to come.

Alongside the gladiators were the *venatores* (also called *bestiarii*), who were considered even lower on the social scale, and who were trained in the *ludus* to fight the wild beasts imported from the provinces. The *venatores* were, like their gladiator counterparts, recruited from slaves, criminals, prisoners of war and those who volunteered. These men were trained by barbarians who had experience in hunting various wild animals in their natural habitats; thus, Parthians taught the use of the bow, Moors the use of the lance, and so on.

Those gladiators who survived long enough came to be what we would call celebrities. The late first century AD poet Martial has this to say of one such gladiator:

> Hermes is the toast of Rome and of his century. Hermes is skilled in the use of all weapons. Hermes is a gladiator and a master of swordsmanship; Hermes strikes fear and terror into his opponents. Hermes knows how to win and win without a blow. There is no one to replace him, except himself.

In the blistering heat of the amphitheatre, the crowds screamed for them, chanting their names in frenzied expectation of the slaughter to come; and when they appeared in the bustling streets, accompanied by a retinue of admiring associates, they invariably caused huge excitement among passers-by.

THE WAGES OF SLAUGHTER

As might be expected, fame was not the only reward for successful gladiators. Although an inexperienced gladiator could not expect to make a great deal of money, a veteran fighter who had proved himself time and again in the arena, and who had retired from combat, could receive a fee of 15,000 sesterces for his re-engagement at a *ludus*. The *lanista* frequently added more money to his payment, the amount depending on the gladiator's degree of popularity. In addition to this, there were times when two particularly skilful gladiators, facing each other in the arena, found their strength and abilities equally matched. They would therefore continue to fight hour after hour, their battle becoming something of a miniature epic. On these occasions, the entertainment and excitement they provided was of such quality that the Emperor could not resist the calls from some parts of the audience that they both be rewarded the *missio*, which meant that they were both sent away with their lives and their honour, to the applause of an appreciative crowd. There was a danger of inciting the displeasure of the crowd if the Emperor kept the men fighting for too long, and so in compensation for this, the Emperor would make a point of giving valuable gifts to each of the gladiators and the longer they fought, the greater became the Emperor's generosity.

Those gladiators who were particularly favoured by an Emperor might even become members of his private circle, and this was when the gifts really started to accumulate. The gladiator Spiculus, for instance, received gifts of astonishing value from Nero. Commenting on this Emperor's attitude to money, Suetonius writes:

> [Nero] never thought twice . . . about giving away or wasting money. He presented Spiculus the gladiator with houses and estates worthy of men who had celebrated triumphs.

Caligula could be equally free and fast with his money, on one occasion giving two million sesterces to the gladiator Eutyches.

However, since the majority of gladiators were slaves, the most valuable reward they could possibly receive was not money or trinkets, but their liberty, and the opportunity to leave behind forever the blood and pain of the arena. This was usually conferred in response to the demands of the spectators, but since a gladiator's worth to his owner grew with his popularity in the arena, the granting of freedom would mean the loss of a very valuable asset, and so slave owners were extremely reluctant to acquiesce to the demands of the people. The final word, of course, belonged to the Emperor, who was quite willing to grant liberty to a successful gladiator . . . although his willingness often evaporated when the slave in question belonged to him.

A VALUABLE POSSESSION

Experienced gladiators, who would put up a good, skilful fight against their opponents and draw the admiration of the crowd were a highly sought-after commodity. One of the reasons *munera* were so very expensive to stage was the high costs charged by the *lanista* for the use of his men, particularly those veterans whose fighting ability had carried them through many hard and bloody battles, and who were well known to the people. Men such as these were money-spinners who could make their *lanista* a very wealthy man. Of course, such were the conditions in the arena that there was always the chance that they might be cut down in the next battle, and an excellent source of income would be lost to the *lanista*. Another reason for the expense of the *munera* was the sheer numbers of gladiators involved. Not every fight turned into an hours-long epic; many were quick and straightforward affairs, with one gladiatior swiftly gaining the upper hand over his opponent, and losing no time in spilling his blood. For example, the spectacles staged by Augustus included an average of 625 pairs of fighters; and Trajan, upon securing victory over the Dacians in AD 106, put on a breathtaking spectacle in which 10,000 men, many of them prisoners of war, were made to fight.

In the early days of the *munera*, the giver of the games went to a *lanista* who rented him the gladiators he needed. This gave the *lanista* quite a lot of clout, at least in financial terms. The *lanistae* made a very healthy living from renting or selling their troupes. There was a considerable disadvantage to this in that they were seen by the citizenry as utterly contemptible, something like an unpleasant cross between a butcher and a pimp, since they earned their living from treating human beings like animals. There was a curious hypocrisy in this attitude, not unlike the ambivalent way in which the gladiatiors themselves were beheld in the eyes of the public, at once scorned and admired. While the *lanistae* may have been the objects of hatred and contempt in Roman society, they still made possible one of that society's favourite pastimes. So their moral objections did not stop the citizenry from enjoying the bloody spectacle of gladiatorial combat on a regular basis. In an extension of this hypocrisy, it was considered acceptable for an upper-class citizen to own a troupe, as long as he remained an amateur dabbler, with his main source of income lying elsewhere.

Even for an aristocratic dabbler, investment in a gladiatorial troupe could be a highly lucrative enterprise: for example, Cicero had a friend named Atticus who made back his investment in a troupe after only two performances. Cicero (106–43 BC), a writer, statesman and orator who would play a key role in the events around Julius Caesar and Octavian, was no lover of the gladiatorial games. In *De Officiis*, the moral treatise he wrote for his son, we read: 'This sort of amusement gives pleasure to children, silly women, slaves and free persons with the characters of slaves; but an intelligent man who weighs such matters with sound judgement cannot possibly approve of them.' Nevertheless he left us much information on gladiators and the ways in which they were perceived in Roman society.

During the Empire, the staging of *munera* was placed under state control, and Imperial *ludi* were set up, becoming the only authorised gladiatorial schools. It was thought unwise to allow private citizens to own and train what could very easily be transformed into a private army. Most gladiatorial troupes were thus placed under the ownership and control of the Emperor. In the early Empire, there were four major training centres. The instruction was very precise, almost scientific, and involved the learning of a series of figures, which were divided into various phases. In fact, a gladiator had to be careful not to follow the training too closely, since the audience would easily spot this and complain that he was fighting too much 'by the book', with no flair or individual style. The four schools were the *Ludus Matutinus*, where those who hunted the wild animals were trained; the *Ludus Gallicus*; the *Ludus Dacicus*; and the *Ludus Magnus*. The last of these was located close to the Flavian Amphitheatre (Colosseum), to which it was linked by an underground passageway. Construction on the *Ludus Magnus* was begun by Domitian and completed by Trajan and Hadrian. It was destroyed by fire during the reign of Marcus Aurelius (AD 161–180), but such was its importance to Roman society that it was very quickly repaired.

We have already seen that life within the gladiatorial schools was no easy ride. Each school contained the inmates' cells and training grounds, together with an arsenal and a forge. Aside from the gladiators themselves, the schools were populated by the trainers, armourers and doctors. These places were bustling miniature communities, whose inhabitants were kept constantly occupied with the business of training the gladiators, cooking their meals, making and maintaining the fearsome weapons, and nursing back to health those who had suffered non-lethal injuries in the arena. The man in charge of administrating each school was known as a *procurator*, a very important individual. Outside Rome, there were many other gladiatorial schools scattered throughout the provinces; unlike in the capital, however, a *procurator* was assigned to oversee the administration of all the barracks within a province, as opposed to individual premises. For example, there was a *procurator per Gallias*, a *procurator per Asiam*, and so on. In Rome itself, the barracks contained up to 2,000 gladiators, although we are less sure how many filled the provincial schools.

During the reign of Marcus Aurelius, and from then onwards, the profession of *lanista* was not as lucrative as it had been, since the state obliged him to supply all his gladiators at a fixed price, and some at a discount. According to Auguet, 'the market for gladiators became a closed one, more or less shackled by regulations based on the principle that "the production of *munera* is a matter of public interest".'

LIFE AND DEATH

Although life in the schools was harsh, it was not so harsh as to harm the physical wellbeing of its inmates. This would not have made sense, of course, since the whole purpose of the schools was to produce the finest possible fighting specimens. The gladiators' diet was good, high in protein and fat, providing essential muscle growth and energy. A good layer of fat would also provide essential protection against sword-cuts, preventing them from slicing muscles and tendons and thus crippling the fighter. The medical care was good, too (or as good as could be expected in the ancient world). They were allowed to form relationships with women, and even to start families (in these cases it is likely that the gladiators were allowed to live outside the *ludus*, in the town).

The gladiators within each barracks formed *collegia* and worshipped the god Hercules. They also frequently forged strong friendships, and lived in a committed and unified community, a kind of microcosm of the world outside. In view of the fact that they would frequently be required to kill each other in the arena, this may sound a little strange; on the other hand, history has taught us repeatedly that extreme adversity can be fertile ground for the growth of powerful friendships and fellow feeling. Whether slaves, prisoners of war or free men, gladiators were companions in adversity, and the bonds they formed, even with men they might one day be required to kill, reflected this.

What happened to gladiators after defeat and death depended on their familial circumstances. Historian Thomas Wiedemann, in his *Emperors and Gladiators* (London, 1996), has investigated the evidence across the lands of the Roman Empire:

Inscriptions from Rome, Puteoli, Padua, Lyon, Nimes, Orange, Cadiz and Salonae in Dalmatia, were erected by gladiators' wives. Other family members are mentioned: a *cursor* [runner] of the *ludus magnus* at Rome, Tigris, was buried by his brother Theonas. At Ostia, the *retiarius* Firmus was buried by his 'brothers' (since he had at least two names, he was presumably a citizen), though that relationship may have been metaphorical. At Brixia, amici bury a gladiator; at Nimes, a fellow-gladiator who buried an *essedarius* made it explicit that the cost for the monument was borne by himself, *de suo*.

As we have seen, the Roman populace's attitude to gladiators was ambivalent in the extreme: while they were reviled as the lowest of the low, gladiators who were skilful and frequently victorious simultaneously enjoyed a heroic status in the eyes of those who attended the games. The most successful gladiators had huge fan-bases, and much screamed support attended their appearance in the arena. We have already seen how women frequently committed the social misdemeanour of visiting the barracks to see their preferred gladiator; young Roman boys also could be found there, taking fighting lessons, on occasion, from their own favourites.

Gladiators would either fight battles between two groups or, more commonly, fight in a sequence of duels. The day before the combat, they were provided with a banquet, called the *cena libera*, which for many of their number would be their last meal on Earth. Some, however, refrained from indulging themselves. There is an interesting passage in one of Plutarch's *Moral Essays* in which he illustrates the difference between the civilisation and rationality of the Greeks, and the savage, irrational behaviour of barbarians. He says that a Greek gladiator, on the eve of his appearance in the arena, would make provision for his wife, if he were married, and the setting free of his slaves, while a gladiator from a barbarian tribe would gorge himself on the *cena libera*.

The next day, the spectacle would begin with a parade. To the cheers and applause of the assembled spectators, the gladiators would march around the arena in military formation, wearing brightly coloured, embroidered clothes. A group of servants would follow them, carrying their weapons. When the parade was over, the weapons would be examined with great care and the best chosen. The pairs of duellists were then chosen by lots and the giver (or *editor*) of the games ordered the duels to begin.

There were many different types of gladiator, each with their own fighting styles and armaments. These different groups had one thing in common, however: they were all, in their own way, deadly.

Gladiators were identified with ethnic names, such as Thracian and Samnite. However, this did not refer to the ethnicity of the men who fought, but rather to the weaponry and fighting techniques of enemy peoples defeated by Rome and then appropriated in the demeaning surroundings of the amphitheatre. Thus, a Thracian gladiator used a round shield and sabre but fought without armour, in the manner of the warriors of Thrace. The Samnite was equipped as the people of Samnium, with an oblong shield, visored helmet and short sword. The Gaul fought with similar armour, but later became known as a *murmillo* (from *mormylos*, a kind of fish) because the crest of his helmet was in the shape of a fish. The *retiarius* (net-man) wore no armour, and used a net to trip and hold his opponent, and a trident to spear him to death. The *essedarii* fought in chariots like the Britons, while the *laquearii* used a lasso to bring their opponents down. The *dimachaeri* carried a short sword in each hand. There was also a type of gladiator known as a *hoplomachus*, from the Greek meaning 'heavily-armed gladiator'.

There were many other types of gladiator, and it is worth looking to William Smith's classic *Dictionary of Greek and Roman Antiquities* (1875) for a few more descriptions of the most important. The *andabatae* wore helmets without any apertures, and thus had to fight blind, a practice the spectators apparently found highly amusing. They would usually fight from horseback, which made their mode of fighting even more difficult and dangerous. The *Catervarii* did not perform in single, man-to-man combat, but rather fought in two teams. This form of combat was not as common as the duels between single gladiators. It could be counted on to produce a great deal of excitement and carnage.

Equites were gladiators who fought on horseback, while the *Postulaticii* were gladiators of various types who were specifically demanded by the spectators from the giver of the games. The *Bestiarii* (who were also known as *venatores*) fought the wild animals, brought from all provinces of the Empire, both near and far. Just as the use of conquered peoples' style of weapons and armour reinforced the Romans' feeling of superiority, so the extraordinary array of wild animals from Asia, Africa and the forests of northern Europe demonstrated the Empire's huge extent.

The origins of these different kinds of gladiators can be traced to the origins of the combats themselves. The Samnites, for instance, are now regarded as a kind of prototype for all the gladiators who would follow. After Samnium's defeat by Rome in 308 BC, the Campanians (who were allies of Rome) captured many Samnite weapons and pieces of armour, and used them to equip the very first gladiators who fought in order to provide entertainment at Campanian feasts. This equipment was adopted by Rome four decades later for its own games.

Samnite armour was both heavy and visually impressive, and remained popular throughout the history of the gladiators. Eventually, though, other types of gladiators were added to the Samnites. The Thracian gladiators were a creation of Sulla (138–78 BC), at least at Rome, for Thracian gladiators appear on Etruscan grave-urns from the third century BC, as do the fighters known as Gauls. There is some confusion here, since some classical sources claim that Gauls were not used until Caesar's Gallic campaigns.

At any rate, the Thracians fought with a curved scimitar,

called a *sica* and a small shield (*parma*), which could be either square or circular. Their legs were fully protected by both *fasciae*, which were tough bands of leather wrapped around the thighs, and greaves around their calves. The Gauls possibly originated in Cisalpine Gaul (the part of ancient Gaul south of the Alps of northern Italy), and were gradually replaced by the *murmillo*, with his distinctive fish-shaped helmet crest.

The *secutor* (or 'pursuer') was another type of gladiator about which little is known for certain. In fact, according to the historian Michael Grant, they are not easy to distinguish from Gauls and *murmillones*, or from another type known as the *provocator*, or 'challenger'. Grant informs us that most of the surviving representations of gladiators belong 'to a general, recognisable type which seems to cover the majority of the various classes'. We can form a basic picture of this type of fighter. He usually had bare thighs and torso, a visored helmet, a rectangular or oval shield, a dagger or short sword, and wore a greave on his left leg (to add to the protection of the shield). He also wore a wide leather or metal belt, which protected his genitals. His right arm, which held the sword or dagger, was protected by the leather bands known as *manicae*. Even those gladiators who wore various pieces of armour frequently had naked torsos. The purpose behind this arrangement was to prolong the fight as much as possible. Without adequate protection on his limbs, a fighter could be quickly incapacitated by a non-lethal blow, which was considered undesirable.

The *secutor*'s usual opponent was the *retiarius*, who fought with a net and trident. Since the *retiarius*' defensive capability was extremely limited (his only piece of armour was the *galerus* which covered his shoulder), one of his most useful tactics was simply to run away from his opponent, darting here and there in the arena until he was able to find an opening for his attack. Although this tactic was quite legitimate and well-understood by the spectators, it still resulted in the *retiarius* being considered the lowest type of gladiator. In fact, this is how the *secutor* (pursuer) got his name. The *retiarius* carried the same equipment as a fisherman, and it was for this reason that the *murmillo*, with the fish-shaped crest upon his helmet, was the usual alternative to the *secutor* as an opponent.

The Roman attitude to the *retiarius'* lack of armour and undignified defensive strategy of flight, resulting in his being considered inferior to other types of gladiator, is quite forcefully displayed in Juvenal's dismissive treatment of a descendant of a noble house who enrolled as a *retiarius*:

> The games! Go there for the ultimate scandal,
> Looking at Gracchus who fights, but not with the arms of a swordsman,
> Not with a dagger or shield (he hates and despises such weapons),
> Nor does a helmet hide his face. What he holds is a trident,
> What he hurls is a net, and he misses, of course, and we see him
> Look up at the seats, then run for his life, all around the arena,
> Easy for all to know and identify. Look at his tunic,
> Golden cord and fringe, and that queer conspicuous arm-guard!

Such was the contempt for the *retiarii* that many of them decided that their particular fighting style was far from satisfactory, and so trained also as Samnites. Suetonius has a peculiar anecdote regarding the behaviour of a group of *retiarii* during a multiple duel in the arena, which incurred the displeasure of Caligula. Having fought very poorly against their *secutor* opponents, they were sentenced to death by the Emperor. Perhaps in an attempt to make amends in professional terms, or perhaps merely to save his own skin, one of the net-fighters took up his trident and, surprising them, killed each of the victorious team.

Caligula then 'publicly expressed his horror at what he called "this bloody murder", and his disgust with those who had been able to stomach the sight.' (This was quite an indictment, coming from Caligula, who was one of the most bloodthirsty and perverted Emperors in history).

The different types of gladiators had their own fans, who would frequently place bets on the outcome of an encounter. Caligula supported the Thracians, and trained as one himself. When watching his favourites in the arena, he could not be counted on to display particularly good sportsmanship. On one occasion, he was watching a fight between a Thracian and a *murmillo*. The *murmillo* defeated the Thracian, but sustained a light wound, into which Caligula poured a deadly poison. This substance he later called Colombinum, after Columbus, the *murmillo* he had killed. It then took pride of place in his rather extensive catalogue of poisons.

The Emperor Domitian's preferences were the other way round and he, also, could become more than a little petulant over his favourite gladiators, the *murmillones*. During one combat in the arena between a *murmillo* and a Thracian (a type of gladiator Domitian particularly disliked), he overheard a citizen remarking that a Thracian might be a match for a *murmillo*, but not for the patron of the games. So indignant was Domitian at this slight to his favourite fighters that he immediately had the offending citizen dragged from his seat, paraded around the arena with a placard tied to his neck, reading 'A Thracian supporter who spoke evil of his Emperor', and then torn to pieces by dogs.

Although the conditions within the gladiatorial schools were harsh, they were very rarely so harsh as to interfere with the development of strong and able fighters. Occasionally, however, the *lanistae* who owned them were very brutal, and conditions in these places were intolerable. The dreadful lives of the gladiators in one such *ludus* gave rise to one of the most famous episodes in ancient history.

CHAPTER FOUR

The Revolt of Spartacus

IV

This book would not be complete without mentioning by far the most famous of all gladiators, a man whose defiance of his brutal masters has become almost legendary: Spartacus. Originally a soldier in the Roman army, Spartacus had deserted and become a brigand. Once recaptured, he had been taken to Rome to be sold into slavery, and eventually found himself in the gladiator school at Capua. Spartacus, though, was not your usual ex-squaddie, as Plutarch writes in his *Life of Crassus*:

> [Spartacus] was a Thracian from the nomadic tribes and not only had a great spirit and great physical strength, but was, much more than one would expect from his condition, most intelligent and cultured, being more like a Greek than a Thracian. They say that when he was first taken to Rome to be sold, a snake was seen coiled round his head while he was asleep and his wife, who came from the same tribe and was a prophetess subject to possession by the frenzy of Dionysus, declared that this sign meant that he would have a great and terrible power which would end in misfortune. This woman shared in his escape and was then living with him.

The gladiators' insurrection led by Spartacus occurred in 73 BC. At that time, life for slaves on the great estates was utterly miserable, with sadistic overseers, inadequate rations and nights spent in chains. For the poor wretches who found themselves in this situation, the only possible prospect of a (marginally) better life lay in joining a gladiatorial troupe. A *lanista* named Lentulus Batiates had a training school in Capua (which for centuries was the headquarters of gladiators) in southern Italy, in which he kept mainly Gauls and Thracians. Unable to bear the brutality of their treatment, some two hundred of these gladiators hatched a plan to escape. The plot was discovered, however, and only seventy-eight were able to pre-empt the actions of their master by raiding the cook's shop, taking various knives and spits and making a break for freedom.

As they made their way through Capua, they came upon a convoy of carts carrying gladiators' weapons, bound for another town, and seized them for themselves. They then chose three captains to lead them, two Gauls named Oenomaus and Crixus, and Spartacus. Once they had seized their freedom, they made their way to Mount Vesuvius, where they established a camp inside the crater, which was not quite as stupid as it sounds, since the volcano was at that time believed to be extinct. From this camp they repulsed the assault that came from Capua. In this engagement they took proper weapons, and contemptuously threw aside their own gladiatorial arms, which they considered to be barbaric and dishonourable. Presently, a commander named Claudius Glaber was despatched from Rome by the *praetor* (magistrate) Publius Varinius to deal with the escaped gladiators. Glaber was accompanied by an army of 3,000 soldiers, which proved no match for Spartacus and his men. Plutarch tells how a stunning victory was achieved:

[Claudius Glaber] laid siege to them in a position which they took up on a hill. There was only one way up this hill, and that was a narrow and difficult one, and was closely guarded by [Glaber]; in every other direction there was nothing but sheer precipitous cliffs. The top of the hill, however, was covered with wild vines and from these they cut off all the branches that they needed, and then twisted them into strong ladders which were long enough to reach from the top, where they were fastened, right down the cliff face to the plain below. They all got down safely by means of these ladders except for one man who stayed at the top to deal with their arms, and he, once the rest had got down, began to drop the arms down to them, and, when he had finished his task, descended last and reached the plain in safety. The Romans knew nothing of all this, and so the gladiators were able to get round behind them and to throw them into confusion by the unexpectedness of the attack, first routing them and then capturing their camp. And now they were joined by numbers of herdsmen and shepherds of those parts, all sturdy men and fast on their feet. Some of these they armed as regular infantrymen and made use of others as scouts and light troops.

Soon Spartacus' band of rebels attracted new recruits, by the hundreds, then thousands, then tens of thousands. After several encounters with Roman forces, each of which saw Spartacus victorious, the rebels decided to turn south towards Metapontum, and then advanced northwards through Italy. When they defeated a Roman army at Mutina (Modena) on the plain of the River Po, the whole of northern Italy was at their mercy. Upon each victory, Spartacus turned the tables of tradition on his enemies, and made his Roman prisoners fight each other to the death as gladiators.

According to Plutarch, Spartacus' intention was to cross the Alps into Gaul and then to Thrace, where the slaves in his band had had their homes, and where they would have secured their freedom once again. However, the band made a fatal – if understandable – mistake: they succumbed to over-confidence. Instead of pushing through to the Alps and on to freedom (which Spartacus himself wanted to do, fully understanding that his own army could not hope to match the might of Rome for very long), the rebels took stock of their victories and decided that their strength was sufficient to take on the Romans. At this point, Crixus left Spartacus, taking the Gaulish and German gladiators with him. Spartacus spent the winter near Thurii (Terranova di Sibari) in Lucania, where he carefully planned his next moves against the Romans.

With the arrival of spring, Spartacus took his men south towards Metapontum, and from there to Bruttium. Soon he heard that the consul Gellius had discovered Crixus' party of Gauls and Germans whose combination of confidence and woeful lack of discipline had caused them to break from Spartacus. He defeated and killed them. Lentulus, the other consul sent to deal with the rebels, was not so successful. He besieged Spartacus with a large army, but was soundly defeated.

In the early twentieth century, Spartacus was held to be a great hero by Marxists. Karl Marx himself said of him that he was the 'finest fellow that the whole of ancient history has to show, a great general . . . a noble character, and a true representative of the ancient proletariat'. However, this is far from the truth. The historian Christian Meier has called Spartacus 'a robber chief on the grand scale', and it is most unlikely that he ever intended to be anything else. Nevertheless, there is no doubt that he and his rebel army were a thorn in Rome's side, terrorising the whole of southern Italy for many months. At the end of 72 BC, after further defeats at the hands of the rebels, Rome placed Marcus Licinius Crassus, the richest man in Rome and one driven by ambition, in charge of the war against Spartacus. After the ignominious defeat of his lieutenant, Mummius (fifty of whose soldiers Crassus had executed for beginning the retreat), Crassus managed to encircle Spartacus with a long trench at the southern tip of the boot of Italy. Spartacus took his men through Lucania towards the sea, where he encountered a band of Cilician pirates. Through his dealings with them, he hoped to strike out to Sicily, from where he could co-ordinate a new phase in the war with Rome. According to Plutarch:

> At the Straits he fell in with some pirate ships from Cilicia and formed the plan of landing 2,000 men in Sicily and seizing the island; he would be able, he thought, to start another revolt of the slaves there, since the previous slave war had recently died down and only needed a little fuel to make it blaze out again. However, the Cilicians, after agreeing to his proposals and receiving gifts from him, failed to keep their promises and sailed off.

When his plan came to nothing, Spartacus had no choice but to fill in the trench at one point and strike out in the direction of Brundisium (Brindisi). Spartacus then suffered a mutiny by some of his followers, who headed off on their own. For them, it was a most unwise decision, for they were soon surrounded and destroyed by Crassus. While Spartacus headed into the mountains of Petelia, Crassus asked the Senate to send the proconsuls Marcus Lucullus (who had commanded Roman forces in Macedonia) and Pompey (who was on his way back from Spain). In the meantime, two of Crassus' officers, Quintus and Scrofas, overtook Spartacus and engaged his forces in battle.

Although Spartacus turned and fought, defeating his pursuers and seriously wounding Scrofas, his victory proved his undoing, for now the rebels were filled with arrogant confidence and were in no mood to continue their withdrawal. They went to Spartacus with their swords in their hands and demanded that he lead them back again through Lucania to face the Romans head-on. Crassus, already encamped nearby, was ready for the attack. In the words of Plutarch: 'Spartacus, seeing there was no avoiding it, set all his army in array, and when his horse was brought him, he drew out his sword and killed it on the spot, saying, if he got the day, he should have a great many better horses of the enemies, and if he lost it, he should have no need of this.' He then made directly for Crassus himself, missing him but slaying two centurions who were converging on him. Finally, finding himself alone, Spartacus stood his ground against his enemies, bravely defending himself until their swords cut him down.

Although Crassus had done most of the hard work in putting down the slave revolt, Pompey took the credit, after intercepting and destroying the last remnants of Spartacus' army. Spartacus, the rebel gladiator, had managed to defeat the armies of Rome no less than nine times, and had forced Rome to mobilise the whole of its military might in order to subdue him.

With Spartacus dead, the remnants of his army were quickly tracked down and terrible examples made of them. Crassus had six thousand captured rebels crucified along the Appian Way that linked Capua with Rome, as a warning to everyone passing along it. Pompey subsequently defeated five thousand rebels who had escaped to the north, and had them all massacred.

The revolt of Spartacus was the only gladiatorial revolt that lasted more than a few days. At Praeneste there was a similar mutiny, but the revolts miscarried. Although at the time Romans panicked, the result was that precautions were quickly put in place against these sort of attempts. There was draconian discipline at the schools, with heavy supervision and the armouries were carefully guarded. In this environment most revolts were doomed from the start. Such was the Romans confidence in these measures that they were not afraid to install the gladiators' schools right in the very centre of the city. Although not forgotten, Spartacus did not frighten the Romans for long.

CHAPTER FIVE

Curio's Swivelling Amphitheatre

Gladiatorial combats were originally held in the Forum, the Circus Maximus and at any other sites providing a sufficiently large central space with room for a few spectators. However, in 53 BC an undistinguished politician named Gaius Scribonius Curio found himself facing a problem familiar to those anxious to win favour with the public: how to stage a *munus* whose magnificence would stun the spectators and elevate him in their eyes? His problem was compounded by the fact that he was not a wealthy man, and he was well aware that *munera* were colossally expensive events to stage. Cicero advised Curio to give up the idea as hopelessly impractical. The story of how Curio solved his problem of providing an astonishing spectacle for the people is told by Pliny the Elder, and it is a most curious tale.

Pliny the Elder, whose full name was Gaius Plinius Secundus, was the foremost scientific authority in ancient Europe. Born in Novum Comum (Como, Italy) about AD 23, he moved to Rome at an early age, and entered the army at 23. After serving in Germany, he returned to Rome in 52, studied jurisprudence, and then devoted himself to writing and scholarly study. Pliny's intense fascination with science had tragic consequences, for when Mount Vesuvius erupted in 79, destroying the cities of Pompeii and Herculaneum, he left Misenum, near Naples, where he was commanding the western Roman fleet, and sailed across the Bay of Naples to Stabiae to examine the volcanic phenomenon more closely. There, he was overwhelmed by the noxious vapours from the eruption, and suffocated.

Pliny's written works reflected his astonishing range of interests. There were historical and scientific works, a treatise on the use of the javelin by cavalrymen, three books on oration (probably written for his nephew, Pliny the Younger), a treatise on declensions and conjugations, a multi-volume history of the Germanic Wars, and 31 books covering Roman history between 41 and 71. He also produced a monumental 37-volume encyclopaedia of art and nature, the *Historia Naturalis*, the first ten volumes of which were published in 77, and the remainder after his death in 79. Compiled from 2,000 books by 100 authors, the encyclopaedia covers subjects such as mineralogy and metallurgy, medicine, horticulture, zoology and botany, anthropology and human physiology, geography, ethnology and astronomy.

According to Pliny, Curio steadfastly ignored the advice of Cicero, and borrowed heavily against the return he hoped to make if his planned *munus* was successful. He then seems to have hit upon an idea for an innovation that would earn the highest approval of the crowd – an innovation not in the *munus* itself, but in the manner of watching it. At this time, little attention was paid to the comfort of the spectators, and there were certainly no permanent buildings in Rome where gladiatorial combats were staged. The practice had been simply to erect large temporary wooden scaffolds on which the audience perched – scaffolds that, moreover, had an unfortunate habit of collapsing when fully laden, causing many deaths and serious injuries. The most famous of these catastrophes, described by Tacitus, occurred at Fidenae during the reign of Tiberius in AD 27.

Unlike his predecessor Augustus, Tiberius, emperor from AD 14 to 37, was no lover of the arena. However, it was not through any humanitarian concerns that Tiberius abstained from attendance at *munera*: it was more because of his opinion that they were a very tedious form of entertainment, fit only for plebeian tastes. Cold and reserved, Tiberius was not popular with the people. Ancient historians wrote of his depravity and cruelty, charges largely dismissed by modern scholars. What is not disputed, though, is Tiberius' disdain for gladiatorial contests. According to Tacitus:

> A gladiatorial display was given in the names of the Emperor's adopted son Germanicus and his own son Drusus. The latter was abnormally fond of bloodshed. Admittedly it was worthless blood, but the public was shocked and his father Tiberius was reported to have reprimanded him. The Emperor himself kept away. Various reasons were given – his dislike of crowds, or his natural glumness, or unwillingness to be compared with Augustus, who had cheerfully attended.

In fact, Tiberius acted sternly on one occasion, when people demanded a gladiatorial spectacle. Suetonius describes what happened:

> Trouble occurred in Pollentia, a Ligurian town at the foot of the Apennines, where the townsfolk would not let the corpse of a leading centurion be removed from the market-place until his heirs had agreed to meet their importunate demands for a free gladiatorial show. Tiberius detached one cohort from Rome, and another from the kingdom of Cottius, to converge on Pollentia, after disguising their destination. They had orders to enter the town simultaneously by opposite gates, suddenly display their weapons, blow trumpets, and consign most of the inhabitants and magistrates to life-imprisonment.

Without Imperial approval, the number of gladiatorial shows fell away, and entrepreneurs quickly spotted a gap in the market.

An ex-slave called Atilius started building an amphitheatre at Fidenae with the intention of mounting a gladiatorial show. But he neither rested its foundations on solid ground nor fastened the wooden superstructure securely. He had undertaken the project not because of great wealth or municipal ambition but for sordid profits. Lovers of such displays, starved of amusements under Tiberius, flocked in – men and women of all ages. Their numbers, swollen by the town's proximity, intensified the tragedy. The packed structure collapsed, subsiding both inwards and outwards and overwhelming a huge crowd of spectators and bystanders. Those killed at the outset of the catastrophe at least escaped torture, as far as their violent deaths permitted. More pitiable were those, mangled but not yet dead, who knew their wives and children lay there trapped with them. In daytime they could see them, and at night they heard their screams and moans.

When the ruins began to be cleared, revealing the crushed and battered corpses, people rushed to them, kissing and embracing the bodies of family members, and even fighting over some, whose features were so mangled as to be unrecognisable, but whose clothes or similarities of physique had caused mistaken identifications. In all, so it is said, 50,000 people were crushed to death or hideously injured in that dreadful catastrophe. The Senate responded with a decree that in future, no one with a capital of less than 400,000 sesterces should be allowed to put on a gladiatorial show, and amphitheatres should be built only upon ground of proven solidity. Immediately after the disaster, leading Romans opened their homes and provided medical attention to the survivors. As Tacitus notes: 'In those days Rome, for all its miseries, recalled the practice of our ancestors, who after great battles had lavished gifts and attentions on the wounded.'

But in Curio's time eighty years earlier there were few rules or regulations to hold back his fertile imagination. His idea was to place two semi-circular wooden stands on pivots, a concept that no one previously had even considered, much less attempted to put into practice. The site could thus perform a double function: in the morning, these stands would be back to back, allowing two different theatrical performances to be presented, without the sounds from either interfering with the other; then, in the afternoon, the two stands would be swivelled around to face each other, forming an oval. Assuming that Pliny's story is true, Curio's swivelling stands are the first known example of an amphitheatre in Rome, although amphitheatres already existed outside the city, notably at Pompeii. Although this is a very unusual and charming story, Michael Grant has his doubts about its authenticity: 'The nature of this mechanical device has been much disputed; but Pliny (or the source of his information) may have made the whole thing up, in a mistaken effort to explain how the word "amphitheatre" came to be invented.'

If, however, the story is true, then it seems that such were the logistical complications involved in the design of Curio's swivelling amphitheatre that no others like it were built. Nevertheless, it had served its purpose in inspiring the construction of a permanent venue for gladiatorial combats in Rome. It also served its purpose for Curio's political ambitions: the colossal debts he had incurred were paid in full by Caesar, who saw in him a potentially powerful ally.

CHAPTER SIX

Realms of Chaos

VI

It was perhaps inevitable that an entertainment as massively popular as gladiatorial combats should eventually be performed in elaborate, purpose-built areas. The makeshift places, such as market squares, had served their purpose in earlier times, but under the Emperors, a new kind of structure appeared, one whose name has become synonymous with death and suffering: the amphitheatre.

Although Curio's swivelling amphitheatre was a brilliant innovation (assuming it actually existed), it did not have the prestige – and permanence – of a stone building. The first such amphitheatre known by us for certain was not constructed at Rome, but in Campania, the country from which it is believed Rome inherited gladiatorial combat. It was built at Pompeii around 80 BC, and had a seating capacity of about 20,000. Its façade was quite low, and the arena itself was dug deep into the ground. This amphitheatre was the scene of the violent brawl between Pompeians and Nucerians, described by Tacitus in Chapter One.

The earliest permanent amphitheatre at Rome was built in 29 BC in the *Campus Martius* by a henchman of Augustus named Titus Statilius Taurus. Partly built of stone and partly of wood, the amphitheatre was destroyed in the Great Fire of Rome in AD 64.

The amphitheatres had a characteristic elliptical shape, the next best thing to a circle, which would have afforded a perfect view of the action for everyone, but would not have allowed any position of authority. Thus, their design was based on the ellipse, on the long curve of which stood the platform reserved for the giver of the games and his entourage.

THE ULTIMATE BATTLEGROUND

The greatest Roman amphitheatre was, of course, the Colosseum, so named because of the colossal statue of Nero that stood nearby. The name 'Colosseum', however, was not applied to this building until the Middle Ages; it was originally called the Flavian Amphitheatre, since it was built by members of the Flavian Dynasty (Vespasian, Titus and Domitian). Dedicated in 80 AD by the Emperor Titus, it could accommodate approximately 45,000 people sitting, and another 5,000 standing.

Beneath the Colosseum was a gloomy labyrinth of passageways and chambers, used to store stage effects and the complex apparatus by which they were raised into the arena. These effects included highly elaborate forest settings with real plants and trees, which were frequently used for the display of exotic animals and the performance of episodes from Greco-Roman mythology. These spectacles were known as *silvae*. In less sophisticated amphitheatres, the creation of these settings took considerable time and effort. Soldiers had the responsibility of uprooting large numbers of trees and other plants and then replanting them in the arena, which had been divided into squares with large wooden beams. A tree was then planted in each of these squares, and a quantity of earth placed over the roots.

In the Colosseum, however, much of this back-breaking work was rendered superfluous by the brilliantly sophisticated machinery installed within its basements. By a system of chains and pulleys, the Roman engineers could make a ready-made forest rise from the ground. The effects could be changed during the course of the entertainments and the crowd would marvel as ornamental shrubs rose up covered with gold to the accompaniment of fountains spraying perfumed water.

Elsewhere in the vast basements of the Colosseum there were cells for the hundreds of wild beasts that would be called upon to fight with the beast-hunters, and to act as dreadful executioners of the condemned criminals who met their ends here.

The platform upon which the Emperor sat with his entourage was called the *pulvinar*, and it was from here that he pronounced judgement on the gladiators who battled beneath him. Directly across from the *pulvinar* was the *tribunal editoris*, upon which sat the magistrates and the holder of the games. There were also special places reserved for the Vestal Virgins, who traditionally attended entertainments, even unthinkably violent ones such as gladiatorial combats. Special accommodation was also reserved for kings and other representatives of foreign nations.

In addition to the enormous area it covered (620 by 513 feet), the Colosseum was unique in that it was four storeys tall, giving it a height of 157 feet. Grant provides us with a description:

> The arches penetrating the three [storeys] nearest to the ground rest upon piers to which are attached three-quarter columns of the Doric, Ionic and Corinthian Orders respectively. The topmost tier is not arcaded: like those beneath, it exhibits the Greek Orders but here they take the form of rectangular engaged columns (pilasters) with Corinthian capitals. Yet these classical Orders are only there to give scale and ornamentation. The essential constructional units are the massive arch-bearing piers, which thus supply an organic link between exterior and interior.

As Grant notes, a height of four storeys was only made possible on this immense scale by the 'epoch-making' invention of concrete.

THE TIERS OF SOCIETY

The seating arrangements inside a Roman amphitheatre reflected the stratification of the society itself. The Emperor and his family, of course, had their own box, from which they watched the carnage unfolding below, with senators and knights occupying their own special sections. Soldiers and civilians sat apart from each other, as did married men and bachelors. Boys sat with their tutors, and women sat with the poorest men in the top tier of the amphitheatre.

In addition to its reflection of Roman society, the amphitheatre also symbolised Rome's image of itself: the battles taking place there represented the victory of civilisation over barbarism, lawlessness and chaos. It was also a place where Roman justice at its harshest was practised. Typically, the form of execution involved sending the criminal into the arena without weapons to face a variety of wild beasts. They, in common with prisoners of war, were also forced to fight each other to the death.

It is ironic that the magnificent Colosseum, a place so closely identified with death, destruction and abject misery, should have bequeathed to the world the means to produce some of its most beautiful and impressive buildings. The principles upon which the amphitheatre was constructed inspired the greatest buildings of the Renaissance, such as Michelangelo's courtyard of the Palazzo Farnese, and the Palazzo della Cancelleria. Both of these buildings contain stones from the Colosseum. Of the Colosseum it was said in the eighth century: 'As long as it stands, Rome will stand; when it falls, Rome will fall; when Rome falls, the world will fall.' Such is the mastery of its construction that it has withstood time's ravages for 2,000 years.

Before moving on, we should pause to note that today the Colosseum has become a symbol of a very different kind. This place, whose original function was so very awful, is brightly lit whenever a death sentence anywhere in the world is commuted.

CHAPTER SEVEN

Duels to the Death

VII

IN THE ARENA

'Everywhere there were wounds, moans, gore; one could only see danger.' Thus, Pseudo-Quintilian in his *Rhetorical Exercises*, describing a gladiator's first experience of the arena. There were many ways for a gladiator to meet his death in the Roman arena, none of them easy. Upon his entrance to the place of battle, such a gladiator would have been immediately aware of two things: first, the bodies of those who had already fought and fallen, their blood mingling with the hot dust of the arena floor; second, he would have heard a sound at least as ominous as the scene of carnage before him – the sound of swords being sharpened. As the whip of the *lanista* drove him on, and the rank smells of sweat and carrion assaulted his nostrils, the gladiator would have seen funeral processions taking away the dead on the couches of Libitina, the Roman goddess of burials . . .

Strange and incongruous as it may seem, gladiatorial contests were attended by musicians, who provided accompaniment to the combat, their music rising and falling in waves as it followed the deadly rhythms of the battle. (The reader may be reminded of the days of silent movies, when every cinema had a piano player who performed much the same service.) Among the instruments played would be a long, straight trumpet called the *tuba*, a water-organ (*organum*) and a large, curved instrument called a *lituus* or *cornu*.

The duels between individual gladiators took place in the afternoon, and, as we have seen, were matches between men with different types of armour and fighting styles. The combat would be refereed by a *lanista*. It has come to be believed by many people that the combats began with the gladiators crying: 'Hail, Emperor! Those who are about to die salute you!' However, there is no evidence that this was common practice among gladiators. As far as we know, the only time this phrase was used was at an event staged by Claudius, as described by Suetonius. On this occasion the gladiators, who were all condemned criminals, said: '*Ave, imperator; morituri te salutant.*' Claudius replied, jokingly: 'Or not.' Understandably desperate, the assembled criminals took this ambiguous comment as a pardon from the Emperor and refused to fight. It is possible that this phrase was used on other occasions, but if so it would only have been used by condemned criminals.

When a contest had reached its bloody end and one of the gladiators lay wounded, he would raise the index finger of his left hand as a sign of submission and request for mercy. Frequently, this would elicit the cry: 'Habet, hoc habet!' ('he's had it!') from the spectators. While it is certainly true that the spectators expressed their judgement with a gesture of the thumb, the popular belief that a thumb turned up meant life and one turned down meant death, is probably a misconception. It is more likely that these gestures had the opposite meaning: up meant death by the sword; down signified an order for the victorious gladiator to drop his weapon. There was, however, one other sign of mercy a fallen gladiator might hope to see: a raised handkerchief.

The gestures of the crowd were not the final word on a gladiator's fate; they were merely recommendations to the *editor* of the games, most often the Emperor himself. The final decision lay with him.

THE DEATH BLOW AND AFTER

If he had fought well and bravely, the defeated gladiator could reasonably expect a *missio* – to be sent away to fight again on another occasion. Some gladiatorial combats were *sine missione,* and in these there was no possibility of reprieve: one gladiator had to die. If a gladiator had not shown sufficient *virtus,* the crowd would almost certainly call for his death. In this event, the defeated gladiator would kneel on the ground facing the victor, and would clasp his thigh. The victorious gladiator would then hold the head of his opponent in his left hand and with his right plunge his sword into his neck.

Although this was the usual method for the *coup de grace,* there are visual representations (such as a relief from Dorres and the Villa Borghese mosaic) which suggest that occasionally the victorious gladiator would plunge his sword into his opponent's back, thrusting it in with both hands.

A defeated gladiator was expected to meet his death bravely. By doing so, he demonstrated to the crowd the triumph of virtue over death. The ritualisation of the whole process in effect put death in its place. The rituals continued after the final blow. Upon the death of a gladiator, an attendant dressed as Charon, the Stygian ferryman, entered the arena and struck the prone fighter with a mallet, possibly symbolising his ownership of the body. He was followed by another attendant, dressed as Mercury, who traditionally escorted the souls of the dead to the underworld. 'Mercury' carried a wand on these occasions, which was in reality a red-hot branding iron, with which he would prod the body of the fallen gladiator. There were two reasons for this: to forestall any attempt by the gladiator to feign death; and to make certain that he was not unconscious.

The dead man was then carried away on a stretcher, or sometimes a long hook would be sunk into his flesh and his corpse dragged away by a horse. He was taken through the Porta

Libitinaria (named after the goddess of burials) on the main axis of the amphitheatre, directly opposite the portal through which he had entered the arena. While this was happening, a group of slaves would restore the arena floor to its original state, turning over the blood-stained sand and removing all gouges and furrows caused by the fighting. By the time they had finished, the arena would appear as if nothing had yet happened there.

When the vanquished had been carried out of the arena, the victorious gladiator would then receive his prize from the *editor*, which might be a crown, a golden bowl or perhaps gold coins. He would also be given the symbol of victory, a palm leaf. These were in addition to the pay he would receive for his appearance at the games.

By this time, the air in the amphitheatre would be dry, stuffy and very dusty, a situation made worse by the presence of the gigantic awning overhead, called the *velarium*, whose purpose was to provide shelter from the sun. Composed of long strips supported by huge wooden masts, the *velarium* was controlled by a system of ropes that could alter the position of the central circular opening. In this way, shelter could be provided for the spectators regardless of the sun's position. Perfumed water was sprayed over the spectators through a system of pipes. When the spectators had thus been refreshed, they were ready to witness the next item on the agenda of carnage.

CHAPTER EIGHT

Battles Upon the Water

VIII

Perhaps the most impressive and elaborate of all gladiatorial displays were the re-creations of naval battles, the *naumachiae*. The word naumachia had two meanings, referring to the nature of the spectacle, and the place in which the spectacle was held; this could be the arena or, alternatively, a purpose built area. The *naumachiae* were among the most complex, elaborate and popular of all the spectacles to be presented in ancient Rome, since the place of battle was flooded with water to a depth sufficient to float ships by means of a system of reservoirs and channels. This incredible expanse of water could just as easily be drained through the same system, a feat which prompted Martial to exclaim in mock surprise: 'There was land until a moment ago. Can you doubt it? Wait until the water, draining away, puts an end to the combats; it will happen right away. Then you will say: the sea was there a moment ago.' The participants in the *naumachiae* were condemned criminals, who were forced to fight each other on the roiling surface of a miniature sea. Although the tendency was for small troupes to fight each other, there were also frequently whole armies of condemned, numbering many thousands.

The hapless criminals (*naumachiarii*) condemned to take part in these displays received no special training, and historians have suggested that it is more accurate to see them simply as mass-executions of rebellious enemies than as gladiatorial contests in the true sense.

The first representation of a *naumachia* was made by Julius Caesar, who had a lake dug in the *Campus Martius* and filled with water for the purpose. The water later became stagnant, and became an unwelcome source of malaria, until Augustus had it drained and filled in. He then dug his own lake near the River Tiber, and surrounded it with a large grove of trees. This was the first permanent site for these 'sea battles'. The vast basin measured 598 yards by 393, and required the construction of an aqueduct 22,000 paces long for the water supply.

The *naumachiae* were frequently re-creations of famous naval battles from history, in particular Greek history, and included a variety of complex conceits, perhaps the most impressive of which was an artificial island, complete with a fort, in Augustus' *naumachia*.

If the staging of *munera* were hugely expensive, they paled to insignificance compared to *naumachiae*, especially those presented in purpose-built venues, which necessitated the diversion of vast amounts of water. That they were staged at all is testament to the young Empire's confidence in itself and the vastness of its resources.

Augustus was the first Emperor (27 BC–AD 14), and his reign saw a period of peace, prosperity and high cultural achievement, known as the Augustan Age. But his rise to power was by no means simple. Born in Rome in 63 BC and originally named Gaius Octavius (Octavian in English), he was the grandnephew of Julius Caesar, who raised him to one of the most important Roman priesthoods, the College of Pontifices, when he was sixteen. When Caesar was assassinated in 44 BC, Octavian learned that he was his adopted heir and changed his name to Gaius Julius Caesar. After Caesar's assassination, and the struggle with Mark Antony, Octavian met with Antony and Antony's ally, the general Marcus Aemilius Lepidus, and formed the Second Triumvirate to rule Rome and its domains. The establishment of the Second Triumvirate resulted in the killing of 500 senators and knights, the triumvirs' enemies. The great orator Cicero was among the victims.

Octavian and Antony then pursued the leaders of Caesar's assassins, Marcus Junius Brutus and Gaius Cassius Longinus, both of whom committed suicide in 42 BC. Two years later, the Roman world was divided between the triumvirs: Octavian took the western provinces, Antony the eastern ones and Lepidus took north Africa. The Triumvirate broke up as a result of Octavian forcing Lepidus from power while Antony was engaged in the campaign against the Parthians.

When Antony married Cleopatra, Queen of Egypt, and recognised Caesarion (her son by Caesar) as her co-ruler, Octavian's position as Caesar's only son was threatened, and war resulted. The forces of Antony and Cleopatra were defeated in a naval battle off Actium in 31 BC, and they killed themselves the following year. Cleopatra's son Caesarion was murdered, and Octavian returned to Rome in 29 BC, the sole ruler of the Roman world.

The Roman Senate gave Octavian the title Augustus ('consecrated' or 'holy') in 27 BC, and bestowed upon him many other titles and powers that had been held by various officials during the Republic. Following the death of Lepidus, he also became Pontifex Maximus, and thus was in control of the state religion. Augustus was a patron of the arts, and maintained friendships with the poets Ovid, Horace and Virgil, and the historian Livy. He was well aware of the political and symbolic importance of the gladiatorial events and brought in a number of changes as Suetonius reports:

He issued special regulations to prevent the disorderly and haphazard system by which spectators secured seats for these shows; having been outraged by the insult to a senator who, on entering the crowded theatre at Puteoli, was not offered a seat by a single member of the audience. The consequent

Senatorial decree provided that at every public performance, wherever held, the front row of stalls must be reserved for senators ... Other rules of his included the separation of soldiers from civilians; the assignment of special seats to married commoners, to boys not yet come of age, and, close by, to their tutors; and a ban on the wearing of dark cloaks, except in the back rows. Also, whereas men and women had hitherto always sat together, Augustus confined women to the back rows ... the only ones exempt from this rule being the Vestal Virgins, for whom separate accommodation was provided, facing the praetor's tribunal.

In addition to his generally benign attitude towards professional entertainers, Augustus banned gladiatorial contests in which the defeated fighter was forbidden to plead for mercy from the crowd and the Emperor (*munera sine missione*). It was characteristic of later bad Emperors to ignore this prohibition, and also to force a victorious gladiator to face another opponent (called a *suppositicus*, or substitute) straight away. The victor's chances of leaving the arena alive were thus greatly reduced. The battles in which multiple gladiators took part (as opposed to man-to-man duels), known as *gregatim*, are also most closely identified with bad Emperors.

Augustus was deified even during his lifetime, and he set the standard for naval displays. Some forty years later the emperor Claudius, determined to match his illustrious predecessor, staged a sea battle representing Sicilians versus Rhodians on the Fucine Lake, involving 19,000 convicts. Once all the spectators were in place, a silver triton rose out of the waters of the Fucine lake, giving the signal for the combat to begin. The spectacle, and its grisly aftermath are described by the historian Tacitus:

The coast, the slopes, and the hill-tops were thronged like a theatre by innumerable spectators, who had come from the neighbouring towns and even from Rome itself – to see the show or pay respects to the Emperor. Claudius presided in a splendid military cloak, with Agrippina in a mantle of cloth and gold . . . A tunnel through the mountain between the Fucine Lake and the river Liris had now been completed. To enable a large crowd to see this impressive achievement a naval battle was staged on the lake itself, like the exhibition given by Augustus on his artificial lake adjoining the Tiber, though his ships and combatants had been fewer. Claudius equipped warships manned with nineteen thousand combatants, surrounding them with a circle of rafts to prevent their escape. Enough space in the middle, however, was left for energetic rowing, skilful steering, charging, and all the incidents of a sea-battle. On the rafts were stationed double companies of the Guard and other units, behind ramparts from which they could shoot catapults and stone-throwers. The rest of the lake was covered with the decked ships of the marines.

Although extremely reluctant to fight at first, they soon got into the swing of things, and fought well and bravely – so bravely that the convicts were rewarded with exemption from immediate execution. But Claudius had overreached himself, as Tacitus goes on to explain:

After the display, the waterway was opened. But careless construction became evident. The tunnel had not been sunk to the bottom of the lake or even halfway down. So time had to be allowed for the deepening of the channel. A second crowd was assembled, this time to witness the infantry battle fought by gladiators on pontoons. But, to the horror of the banqueters near the lake's outlet, the force of the out-rushing water swept away everything in the vicinity – and the crash and roar caused shock and terror even farther afield.

Claudius' successor Nero staged a naval battle featuring Athenians and Persians at the inauguration of his new amphitheatre in AD 57; it is interesting that, after the battle had ended, the water was drained away, and there followed a gladiatorial show held on dry land.

If anything could eclipse the spectacle of the *naumachia* itself, then it had to be the speed with which an arena could be flooded and drained, this completely altering the scene before the astonished eyes of the spectators. The most elaborate example of this engineering flexibility was perhaps displayed by Nero, who staged a hunt in the arena, then flooded it for the presentation of a *naumachia,* then drained it for an afternoon of gladiatorial combats, and finally flooded it again in order to give a banquet for the spectators on board a ship.

The use of water remained a popular novelty. At the inauguration of the Colosseum in 80 AD, Titus had water pour into the arena; the various animals who were in it had all been taught to swim. There followed a battle between Corcyreans and Corinthians. On another occasion Titus had Athenians fight Syracusans, both sets re-enacting battles of the Peloponnesian war as described by Thucydides.

Titus' successor Domitian was also keen to emulate the successes of Augustus and, as Suetonius notes, ' A lake was dug at his orders close to the Tiber, surrounded with seats, and used for almost full-scale naval battles, which he watched even in heavy rain.' Sometimes, his *naumachiae* didn't quite come off, either. In the *naumachia* which Domitian held in the Circus to celebrate a German triumph, most of the participants lost their lives as the result of a sudden storm.

Naumachiae were not presented as regularly as the *munera,* and are not mentioned in the classical literature after the first century AD. It is likely that expense, in manpower as well as in materials, caused them to fade away. But while they lasted, we might call them the Roman prototype of the historical epics of our own cinema of the 1940s, '50s and '60s.

Spectacular as they were, the *naumachiae* were extensions of the combats between gladiators. The screams of the dying amid gouts of blood were not enough for the plebeians of first-century Rome: they required something more, something to make the carnage more interesting, for they quickly tired of the commonplace, even when it included slaughter on a fantastic scale.

There was, however, another form of combat that became hugely popular with the jaded spectators; one that had nothing to do with the pitting of one fighter against another on more or less equal terms. In these battles, man did not face man: he faced wild beasts.

CHAPTER NINE

Battles Against the Beasts

ORIGIN OF THE NIGHTMARE

The *venationes* (or 'hunts') originally took place in the morning, as a kind of additional feature complementing the main attraction, which was the gladiatorial *munus* of the afternoon. The hunts were even more cruel and bloodthirsty than the man-to-man combat. During the last two and a half centuries of the Republic, there was a growing interest in provinces such as North Africa. The *venationes* began as straightforward exhibitions of exotic animals; for example, Caesar was instrumental in bringing the first giraffe to Rome, an act that won him great praise. Augustus was fond of displaying in the Forum strange beasts sent to him by the governors of distant provinces. However, eventually the sight of unusual animals grew tiresome to the Roman people, and it was decided that the best way to spice up the displays would be to slaughter them.

So in the first century BC, the display of exotic wild animals was replaced by the *venatio*. As its popularity grew, the *venatio* came to be held in the afternoon, the Roman equivalent of 'prime time' viewing. As with gladiatorial contests, the hunts were first held in the Forum, the *Saepta* (an area of the *Campus Martius* normally used for voting) and in the *Circus Maximus*, which was normally used for chariot racing. These areas had not been designed for the presence of dangerous wild animals, and so certain necessary modifications had to be made, such as a ditch around the arena to protect the crowd from any ferocious beasts trying to escape. The Flavian Amphitheatre (Colosseum), on the other hand, was a much safer structure. A thirteen-foot-high podium with smooth walls kept the animals well away from the spectators. As an additional precaution, nets were strung around the perimeter of the arena to prevent any big cats from leaping into the crowd. Although this hindered the view a little, it is unlikely that anyone complained.

The unfortunate beasts themselves, whose destiny it was to meet their deaths here, were kept in cages in underground cubicles beneath the circumference of the arena. The cubicles were raised with ropes and pulleys to openings in the podium, and the beasts were released into the arena. Once out of their cubicles, the animals' only means of retreat was cut off by the raised door sliding back. Sometimes, the noise of the baying crowd terrified even the most powerful and dangerous of animals, so that they steadfastly refused to enter the arena. When this happened, people known as *magistri* would be called upon to throw burning straw into the cubicle to drive them out. These men also had the unenviable task of retrieving those animals that had not been killed.

BEAST VERSUS BEAST, BEAST VERSUS MAN

The wild beast displays took three principal forms. Firstly, various animals were pitted against each other in fights to the death, which were supposed to be illustrative of the primal chaos of the natural world, and its subduing and control by Roman might. Secondly, the *bestiarii* ('wild beast fighters', who were also known as *venatores*) entered the ring to hunt them with a variety of weapons. The animals were usually killed, but occasionally they defeated the hunter, and the blood that flew in gouts was human blood. The Colosseum became the primary site for these spectacles. As the name suggests, the hunt consisted of men stalking the animals through the arena. In the first century

BC, Caesar sent five hundred infantrymen into the arena against about five hundred elephants. Cicero writes of the magnificence of events such as this, but adds: 'What pleasure can there be for a civilised man when either some powerless man is ripped to shreds by a powerful beast or some magnificent animal is transfixed by a spear?'

THE ELEPHANTS' LAMENT

Indeed, the spectators themselves reacted in a most ambivalent way to an episode during the games given a few years earlier in 79 BC by Pompey, in which twenty African elephants were pitted against people of the Getuli, an African nomadic tribe. The hunting technique of the Getuli involved aiming a spear at the lower eyelids of the elephants. When it hit its target, the spear penetrated the animal's skull, entered the brain and killed it instantly. When the hunters had slaughtered several of these magnificent and noble beasts, the surviving elephants charged at the iron grilles that had been specially installed around the perimeter of the arena. Their attempt to escape failed, and the elephants then staggered back to the centre of the arena, and died in abject agony.

The spectators then rose to their feet and started to hurl abuse at Pompey. According to Dio Cassius:

The elephants had withdrawn from the combat covered with wounds and walked about with their trunks raised towards heaven, lamenting so bitterly as to give rise to the report that they did not do so by mere chance but were crying out against the oaths in which they had trusted when they crossed over from Libya and called upon heaven to avenge them! It was recalled that they had refused to board the ships before they received a pledge under oath from their drivers that no harm should come to them.

Some historians have suggested that the crowd's reaction to what they had seen displayed a certain tenderness towards the elephants that had been so cruelly slaughtered, an intuitive understanding of their intelligence. This, however, is unlikely: it is much more feasible to ascribe the crowd's berating of Pompey to fear induced by the elephants' sudden charge at the grilles surrounding the arena. At any rate, elephants continued to be slaughtered in Roman amphitheatres, and Caesar saw no risk of unpopularity when he sent his 500 elephants to meet their ends.

CONDEMNED TO TOOTH AND CLAW

In the third and final form the beast displays took, men and women condemned to death were forced into the arena to face the beasts. Like the voluntary fighters, who went into the arena with weapons and armour (and who usually came off best against the animals), the condemned criminals were also called *bestiarii*; however, unlike the voluntary fighters, it was their fate to do battle against the wild beasts without the benefit of either weapons or armour. In these cases, the outcome was something of a foregone conclusion. The punishment was called *ad bestias* ('to the beasts') and was considered, along with crucifixion, to be the most shameful of all punishments. It was thus considered the best penalty for slaves and lower-class citizens; upper-class citizens were usually beheaded by sword. Christians were thrown to the beasts because their refusal to acknowledge the gods of the state was considered a particularly heinous crime. We shall have more to say on this unpleasant and bloody matter in the next section.

A GORY DIVERSION

While the *venationes* developed from the original exhibitions of exotic animals (which were not slaughtered), this element was retained in later times, and was an attraction very similar to our own circuses, with the animals trained to perform various tricks. The Romans, however, drew no distinction between watching an animal perform an amusing trick and watching it being slaughtered or slaughtering an unfortunate human being: for them, these were all elements of the same type of spectacle, the *venatio*.

The populace was eager to witness the struggles of the jungle (or what they assumed to be the struggles of the jungle), and many different animals were forced to fight each other in the arena, and to meet their ends in this terrifying, hot, dusty and alien place. One of their favourite wild beasts was the magnificent rhinoceros with its natural heavy armour, although they found its essentially peaceful nature frustrating on occasion. When a rhinoceros failed to charge its opponents (which included elephants, bulls and bears), the *magistri* attempted to infuriate it by prodding it with lances. Sooner or later this did the trick, and once the animal lost its temper, nothing could withstand its onslaught. Bulls were eviscerated like straw dummies and the bears were thrown into the air like puppies.

Particularly popular were pairings such as that between the lion and tiger, the bull and wild boar and, more perversely, bears and pythons, lions and crocodiles, and seals and bears. Frequently, two animals would be chained together. In a combination of panic induced by being cast into the arena, with its thousands of baying spectators, and frustrated rage at their inescapable attachment to each other, the poor beasts would fly at each other, causing hideous injuries. The philosopher and dramatist Seneca tells us of one such spectacle involving a bull and a panther whose close proximity to each other drove them into a frenzy in which they ripped each other to shreds. Eventually, armed men (*confectores*) approached the two mangled but still living heaps and finally released them from their misery.

THE BEAST-FIGHTERS

The usual weapon with which the *venatores* faced their adversaries was a long hunting spear with an iron point on the end. This could either be used as a harpoon, or as a defensive weapon against a beast's charge. Some *venatores* wore no armour, being dressed only in a tunic and wearing leather bands on their arms and legs, while others wore iron plates over their chests and flared shoulder guards similar to the *galera* worn by the *retiarii* or net-fighters. Others wore coats of mail that completely covered them, similar to the *andabatae*. While this might have seemed the best option when dealing with a ravenous wild beast, these *venatores* had only a sword with which to fight, and so could only engage the animal at close quarters. When faced with a bull or rhinoceros, such a fighter would frequently be in danger of being crushed to death.

Some particularly tough men disdained the use of weapons altogether, and fought the beasts with their bare hands. It has been suggested that these types opted for stunning a bear with a single blow to the snout before choking the life out of it, or for choking a lion to death by thrusting an arm down its throat. They also frequently used a tall wooden device called a *cochlea*, which the *venator* could spin around on its vertical axis, similar to a modern revolving door, and thus disorient and confuse an enemy while simultaneously avoiding its teeth and claws. Other spectacles were known as the *missiones passivae*, in which a group of *venatores* faced a large assortment of animals. Such battles could be expected to be particularly ferocious and bloody.

There were also bullfights (a spectacle that has found its way down to us in the modern world, for better or worse). In this case the fighters were known as *taurarii*, and fought the bulls with lances and pikes. A variation on this (borrowed from the Thessalians) involved an unarmed fighter riding around the arena on horseback, with the bull in hot pursuit. Eventually, the beast would tire itself out, whereupon the fighter would fling himself from his horse's back to the bull's and attempt to throw it to the ground by twisting its neck.

A LIVING CARGO

These spectacles required a truly fantastic number of animals to be brought to Rome from the farthest corners of her territories. It is said, for instance, that 9,000 beasts were slaughtered during the inauguration of the fabulous Colosseum. While figures such as this may be exaggerations on the part of classical authors, it is certainly true that prodigious numbers of animals were needed to satisfy the public's thirst for exotic blood, particularly when we recall that the practice of *venationes* continued for approximately seven hundred years. The Roman taste for the bizarre and unusual had a disastrous effect on certain species; the historian Auguet mentions 'the progressive disappearance of a degenerated variety of elephant which inhabited north Africa until its final extinction in the fourth century AD, and the growing scarcity of lions in those same districts where, it is said, they had formerly been so numerous as to beleaguer native villages.'

Exotic animals were imported from North Africa and the Near East. Those who were despatched to gather the animals were immediately faced with a very considerable problem: how to trap and subdue a wild (often man-eating) beast. The wild-beast hunts of the arena were thus preceded by highly eventful expeditions to remote and exotic lands, resulting in many dangerous adventures, which must have been at least the equal of the events in the amphitheatre. The hunters utilised a variety of methods to secure their quarry, usually gleaned from the indigenous peoples of the areas in which they operated. For instance, to trap a lion or panther, a pit would be dug and a wall built in front of it. A small animal such as a dog would then be tied to the wall. Attracted by the sounds of the dog barking, the big cat would jump over the wall and straight into the pit. The hunters then lowered a cage containing some form of bait into the pit and enclosed the cat within it. There seems also to have been an alternative method of securing large cats: upon discovering a pool from which the predators drank, the hunters would pour large amounts of wine into it. When the cat drank from this pool, it became helplessly drunk, and was thus handled with the greatest of ease.

The hunters also took very young cats, fending off their enraged mother with lances and shields. Once they had collected the cubs, they would then ride their horses at full gallop towards the gangplank of a ship waiting on the bank of a river. If they mother cat got too close to the horse, and threatened to bring it down, the rider would simply toss one of the cubs over his shoulder. The mother would then stop and take her offspring back to her den. The purpose of this was to ensure a supply of animals that could be tamed and made to perform the various tricks (including the devouring of human beings) which the Roman people found so diverting.

Of course, such was the perilous nature of the job at hand that not everyone could expect to return alive from these adventures. The ferocious struggles to secure wild beasts have been immortalised on a number of mosaics, which show hunters lying on the ground, their shields protecting them (for how long we do not know) from the jaws of lions and tigers. Others show hunters who have let fly their javelins at some ravenous beast, only to miss and thus be faced with the unenviable task of defending themselves with their bare hands. In cases such as this, the hunter's life would most certainly rest in the hands of his companions, who would rush forward with burning torches or other weapons, and would drive the snarling animal back – assuming, of course, that they were able to come to his aid before the beast reduced him to a mass of quivering chunks.

There were a number of other techniques for capturing wild and dangerous animals. One Numidian method was to surround the animal and drive it into an enclosure composed of branches strengthened by nets. The hunters would then surround the entrance to the enclosure with torches, which they would thrust in the face of the hapless creature, preventing its escape. At this stage, the speed and confusion inherent in the hunt resulted in a variety of animals – from ostriches to carnivores – being imprisoned in the same enclosure, an obviously unsatisfactory arrangement, which resulted in the death of many valuable animals. The different species were thus separated and placed in different enclosures as quickly as possible.

When a hunt had been completed, the animals were placed in sturdy wooden cages reinforced with metal bands. Once they were confined within these dark prisons, the animals usually calmed down a little, which was just as well, since they would surely otherwise have dashed themselves to death in desperate attempts to escape. The massive cages were then placed on carts drawn by oxen. If the animals had been captured on the European mainland, they would have made the entire journey to Rome in this manner; if they had been caught in Africa, however, their great wooden prisons would have been transferred to a ship, and an even more traumatic stage of their journey would then begin. This method of transportation was all well and good for smaller beasts, but it quickly became a logistical nightmare when extremely large, heavy beasts such as elephants and rhinoceroses were involved.

The hunting of elephants presented its own set of problems, not least of which was their intelligence. Although, like the big, dangerous cats, elephants were frequently lured into pits, it seems that their brain-power got the better of their hunters. Other elephants frequently came to their aid, partially filling in the pit with loose earth, which they moved with their feet. The trapped elephant was then helped out by its fellows, to the astonishment of the hunters.

When they did manage to secure one of these magnificent beasts, the hunters' problems continued. As with the lion hunts, these events are represented on mosaics, one of which, found at Veii, provides a splendid illustration of just how difficult the transportation of an elephant could be. The scene is of a ship moored to a quay, either on a coast or the bank of a river. A group of men can be seen busying themselves, near the prow of the vessel, with the task of getting an elephant on board. A narrow gang-plank has been lowered, and the elephant has just begun, with obvious trepidation, to mount it. Its feet are bound by ropes secured to the bulwarks which serve a double purpose: to pull the animal towards the ship, and also to control the placing of its feet so that it does not lose its footing on this unfamiliar surface.

Although we know little of the conditions endured by the animals on these voyages, we can imagine the terror and confusion they must have felt, as their strange new surroundings heaved and swayed upon the waves. These must have been strange voyages indeed, for the sailors as much as for their living cargo, with all manner of wails, grunts and roars issuing from their fragile, solitary ship as it floated upon the Mediterranean. The literature of the time captures such a scene well:

> A noise rises from the depths of the abyss; all the giants of the sea rush towards it; Nereus matches with his monsters the monsters of the land . . . A serpent on the yards slithers drunkenly, a lynx leaps onto the rigging sprinkled with wine, and the tigress casts astonished glances at the sails . . .

The capture of wild animals and their transportation to Rome during the Republic was handled by the magistrates who organised the *venationes* in the arena. When they needed animals, they contacted the provincial governors, for instance in Africa or Asia, and informed them of their requirements. The governors then informed merchants or native hunters of what was required, the animals were captured, and the long journey to Rome then began.

During the Empire, things were somewhat different. So popular were the *venationes* that the capture of wild and exotic animals became fantastically expensive. Where private enterprise had previously controlled the whole business, the state now took over, and established an incredibly elaborate system. The task of capturing the animals fell to the various legions stationed at the limits of the Empire; indeed, many Roman soldiers were exempted from regular duties so that they might devote themselves full-time to the securing of wild beasts for the amphitheatres. For example, Legion I Minervia, which was quartered near Cologne, occupied itself with the capture of wild bears.

There were, of course, many provincial towns between the site of the capture and Rome, and these served as stages at which the animals were rested and fed during their traumatic journey. To make the trip in a single stage would have proved very hazardous to the health of the animals, which for the most part were destined to die at Rome.

THE MENAGERIES

Such was the expense and logistical complications of securing wild beasts that menageries were established at Rome, in which huge numbers of animals were kept in preparation for their appearance and slaughter in the arena. These menageries were an essential possession of the Emperor, since they contained an enormous variety of beasts, which he could use whenever the need arose. In this way he was spared the vicissitudes of purpose-driven hunts, with all their attendant complications regarding capture and transportation. In addition, any beast which arrived at Rome in a state of illness or weakness caused by its arduous journey could be nursed back to health and made ready for its slaughter. Many animals suffered badly from changes in temperature and diet, to say nothing of the diseases that could easily spread amongst them during their long confinement. Elephants were usually taken by river to parks at Ardea. Another menagerie was located at Laurentum.

During the time of Augustus, no less than 3,500 animals were kept in the Emperor's menagerie in a fifteen-year period. According to Auguet: 'Of these, 400 were tigers, 260 lions, 600 panthers, as well as other animals of all sorts: seals, bears, eagles, etc.' The cost of maintaining these beasts was enormous, considering the administration that was required. Their capture was merely the first stage; they had to be transported, fed and trained for the various tasks they would be required to perform in the arena. So great was the expense incurred in the provision of *venationes* that the treasury was occasionally burdened quite intolerably, and the Emperor had little choice but to give away parts of his menagerie as gifts.

While it might appear the very essence of cruel frivolity, the *venatio* actually served three important cultural purposes in ancient Rome. Firstly, just as the *munera* were intended partly to display the domination by Rome of its enemies, the *venatio* demonstrated the mastery of civilised Romans over the wild and chaotic forces of Nature, to reinforce in the minds of its people the position of Rome as the greatest and most powerful civilisation the world had ever known. The *venatio* reassured them that nothing on Earth could stand in the way of their domination of the world. Let the forces of Nature be unleashed in all their savagery; they would still quail before Rome. For instance, bulls were frequently hunted and killed in the arena – the bull being a familiar symbol of savagery in the Mediterranean world.

Secondly, the *venatio* was an extension of the widespread performance of sacrificial rituals in that polytheistic society, although in later times the religious undertones would be all but subsumed by the desire for astonishing entertainment. Thirdly, the *venatio* served a democratising function similar to the Emperor listening to the complaints of the crowd. In all ancient cultures, including Rome, hunting was exclusively an aristocratic activity, and the *venatio* offered the common people an opportunity to participate in an activity from which they were otherwise excluded. Under the Empire, this inclusion of the plebeians in the hunt (at least in that they were allowed to witness it from the tiers of the amphitheatre) was all the more illusory – as illusory as the representations of wild Nature displayed in the *silvae*.

As Wiedemann notes, in the ancient world it was considered perfectly natural for human beings to dominate animals, to do with them as they pleased. This attitude was powerfully influenced by the concept of *reason* as the principal characteristic distinguishing adult males from beings such as slaves, barbarians, children and animals, with all of whom it was impossible to reason. One of the most influential proponents of this view was the philosopher and dramatist Seneca (4 BC ? – AD 65).

Trained in philosophy and rhetoric at Rome, Seneca was deeply influenced by the teachings of the Stoics. In AD 49 he was made a praetor, and became Nero's tutor. The first five years of Nero's rule were characterised by clemency and moderation, and this was due in no small part to Seneca's influence. This influence, however, was not to last, and Nero, jealous of Seneca's wealth, tried unsuccessfully to have him poisoned. By this time, Seneca had retired, and was devoting himself to writing.

Seneca himself, with a firm belief in the hierarchy of man, child and beast, had no compunctions against cruelty to animals:

THE GLADIATOR

Children and adults are alike deceived, but adults in different and more important things. Therefore the wise man will treat an insult from such a foolish person as a joke, and sometimes, if they were children, he would tell them off and inflict humiliation and punishment on them, not because he has received an injury, but because they have tried to do one, and to deter them in future. That is the way we deal with animals, using the whip . . .

CHAPTER TEN

The Emperors Who Fought as Gladiators

Earlier in this book we saw how curious was the ambivalence with which Romans regarded the gladiators and *bestiarii* who fought in the arena. On the one hand, they were considered the lowest of the low, cursed with a status in society beneath even that of the slave. And yet, they were also what would be called in modern parlance 'celebrities' or 'superstars', admired by men and young boys, adored and lusted after by women. Some even found their way into an Emperor's inner circle, where they would receive gifts valuable enough to assure them security for the rest of their lives. Nowhere is this strange ambivalence more forcefully represented than in the habit of some Emperors of actually entering the arena themselves and taking on the role of gladiator or *bestiarius*.

The Emperor Nero was especially fond of making a spectacle of himself in this way, caring nothing for the reaction this would provoke. On one occasion, he decided to take on a lion in the arena, but not before it had been suitably 'prepared', so to speak, so that by the time it faced the Emperor, it was in no fit state to stand, let alone fight, and was easily despatched.

Although many Emperors of sound mind took to the arena, including Titus and Hadrian, we may focus our attention on two in particular, who were most definitely *not* of sound mind: Caligula and Commodus.

CALIGULA

Caligula's name has become synonymous with cruelty and perversion of the most bestial kind. Caligula's real name was Gaius Julius Caesar Germanicus; 'Caligula' was a nickname meaning 'little boot', given to him when he was a small boy with his father, the Roman general Germanicus Caesar, in the army camps. He is, of course, legendary for his arbitrary ruthlessness and instability. He hated the nickname, and anyone who used it in his presence could expect some very rough treatment indeed. He positively enjoyed inflicting suffering on others, so much so that he would order men to be killed so that he could watch them closely and actually try to feel they were dying.

Suetonius has an awful little anecdote regarding Caligula's rather vile sense of humour, and how those upon whom it was wielded were almost certain to suffer in some bizarre and outrageous way:

> As an example of his sense of humour, he played a prank on Apelles, the tragic actor, by standing beside a statue of Jupiter and asking: 'Which of us two is the greater?' When Apelles hesitated momentarily, [Caligula] had him flogged, commenting on the musical quality of his groans for mercy. He never kissed the neck of his wife or mistress [he committed incest with his three sisters] without saying: 'And this beautiful throat will be cut whenever I please.'

Caligula was born in AD 12, probably at Antium (now Anzio), and was Emperor from 37 to 41. He was the grandnephew of the Emperor Tiberius. Although Tiberius named both his grandson, Tiberius Gemellus (19–38) and Caligula as joint heirs to the throne, the Roman Senate and the people chose Caligula as sole ruler. Caligula adopted Gemellus as his son, but later had him murdered.

He quickly squandered his vast fortune (which was said to be in excess of 2,300 million sesterces, a truly colossal sum) on public entertainments and vast, unlikely building projects, which at first endeared him to the populace. However, it quickly became apparent that he was seriously unstable (if not completely insane). When his fortune had been spent, which took about a year, he began to dream up new ways of taxing the people, and his popularity fell dramatically. New taxes were levied on the most absurd and outrageous pretexts. Everything that could be bought was subject to an added tax, including foodstuffs. A charge of 2½ per cent was imposed on all legal transactions and law-suits. Ordinary people had to give over one eighth of their daily earnings, and prostitutes had to hand in their fee for a single sexual act – even if they had quitted their profession and were married.

On one occasion, he re-decorated a suite of rooms in his Palace, turned it into a brothel and filled it with married women and free-born boys, then invited all men to come and partake. Those who arrived were lent money to enjoy themselves – at interest, of course. He enjoyed gambling, and as might be expected was both a cheat and a liar. One evening, during a game of dice, he stood up and offered his chair to the man standing behind him. He then went out into the courtyard, where he encountered a pair of rich knights who were out for a stroll. Caligula immediately had them arrested, confiscated all their property, and then went back inside to resume the game.

Another method he used to swell his coffers was to auction properties belonging to those people he had executed (which were numerous). On one occasion, the senator Aponius Saturninus fell asleep during an auction. Caligula noticed this, and told the auctioneer to keep an eye on the senator who kept nodding his head. By the time he woke up, Aponius had unwittingly bought thirteen gladiators, costing 90,000 gold pieces.

Suetonius had plenty to say about Caligula:

[H]e could not control his natural cruelty and viciousness, but he was a most eager witness of the tortures and executions of those who suffered punishment, revelling at night in gluttony and adultery, disguised in a wig and a long robe, passionately devoted besides to the theatrical arts of dancing and singing, in which Tiberius very willingly indulged him, in the hope that through these his savage nature might be softened. This last was so clearly evident to the shrewd old man, that he used to say now and then that to allow Gaius to live would prove the ruin of himself and of all men, and that he was rearing a viper for the Roman people and a Phaethon for the world.

The following are special instances of his innate brutality. When cattle to feed the wild beasts which he had provided for a gladiatorial show were rather costly, he selected criminals to be devoured, and reviewing the line of prisoners without examining the charges, but merely taking his place in the middle of a colonnade, he bade them be led away 'from baldhead to baldhead'. A man who had made a vow to fight in the arena if the Emperor recovered, he compelled to keep his word, watched him as he fought sword in hand, and would not let him go until he was victorious, and then only after many entreaties. Another who had offered his life for the same reason, but delayed to kill himself, he turned over to his slaves, with orders to drive him through the streets decked with sacred boughs and fillets, calling for the fulfilment of his vow, and finally hurl him from the embankment. Many men of honourable rank were first disfigured with the marks of branding-irons and then condemned to the mines, to work at building roads, or to be thrown to the wild beasts; or else he shut them up in cages on all fours, like animals, or had them sawn asunder. Not all these punishments were for serious offences, but merely for criticising one of his shows, or for never having sworn by his *Genius.*

Caligula's bestial nature indeed knew no bounds. Such was his taste for cruelty – psychological as well as physical – that he made parents attend their sons' executions. When one father, unable to face the horror of witnessing his son's death, excused himself, claiming that his health was not good enough to allow him to attend, Caligula provided a litter for him. On another occasion, he invited another father to dinner just after the son's execution. He then made a sickening display of friendliness, and attempted to make the distraught father laugh and joke. He watched the manager of his gladiatorial and wild-beast shows being flogged with chains for several days running, and only decided to put the man out of his misery when the smell from the brains seeping out through his cracked skull became intolerable. A writer of Atellan farces was burned alive in the amphitheatre, because of a line that had an amusing *double-entendre*. One knight was condemned to be thrown to the wild beasts in the arena. At the last moment before being hurled towards his fate, he screamed at Caligula to have mercy upon him, for he was innocent. Caligula halted the proceedings, had the knight taken out of the arena, and had his tongue ripped out before ordering that the sentence be carried out as planned.

It was horrendously easy to incur Caligula's displeasure: having a fine head of hair was enough to do it. Caligula himself was bald, and whenever he came across an attractive man with nice hair, he had him seized and his scalp shaved (considering the Emperor's sexual proclivities, such men probably thought they had got off lightly). A centurion's son, named Aesius Proculus, was famous in Rome for being very well-built and extremely handsome, so much so that the people called him 'Giant Cupid'. During a spectacle, Caligula decided to order Aesius to be dragged from his seat and sent into the arena. He was forced to fight first a *retiarius* and then a *secutor*. When

Aesius won both of these combats, Caligula decided that the only thing for it was to have him executed, whereupon he was dressed in rags, bound and led through the streets like the most pitiful of slaves. Women jeered at him as he was dragged towards his death.

Caligula also frequently appeared in the arena as a gladiator, specifically as a Thracian, with a round shield and sabre, but without armour (not that he needed any). He also had a curious habit of constructing strange buildings inspired by abstract ideas. In fact, the stranger the construction project, the more attractive it was to him. He is said to have had flat plains raised to the height of mountains, and mountains hacked away until all that remained were flat plains. He had tunnels excavated through hard rock for no reason whatsoever (one of the reasons his vast fortune lasted only one year). Auguet provides two more examples:

[T]o give visual and palpable material form to the symbolic identity established by his predecessors between the Emperor and the gods, he had the Capitol, the temple of Jupiter (whose equal he was especially anxious to prove himself) connected to his own house by a bridge 'which overtopped the temple of the divine Augustus'. On another occasion he had built on the sea between Baiae and Pozzuoli a bridge two and a half miles long, made up of a double row of boats which was then covered with earth, giving the whole 'the aspect of the Appian Way'. History does not say if he also planted trees. When the work was finished, the Emperor, dressed as a Thracian gladiator, rode over the bridge, from one end to the other, mounted on a richly caparisoned horse, and was then borne across it in a chariot drawn by two famous horses, this time dressed as a charioteer. This lasted two days.

Suetonius provides the answer to this apparently lunatic

behaviour: the astrologer Thrasyllus had previously eased the worries of Tiberius by claiming that Caligula had no more chance of becoming Emperor than of crossing the bay of Baiae on horseback. Caligula had already proved that prophesy false by becoming Emperor; but he wanted to refute it a second time by actually performing the feat Thrasyllus had considered to be of equal unlikelihood.

Suetonius does not restrain himself in giving examples of Caligula's rather dubious sense of humour, which almost invariably involved a good deal of suffering for someone. For instance, during gladiatorial shows he would order that the canopies that provided shelter from the fierce heat of the sun be removed, and then forbid anyone to leave the amphitheatre. The people then had a simple choice: swelter or die. He was also fond of pitting ageing, weak former gladiators against decrepit wild animals. Even more disturbingly, he staged comic duels between members of respectable families who suffered from various physical disabilities. On more than one occasion, he closed down the granaries and let the people go hungry.

His sexual exploits are, of course, legendary. He was accused of being both an active and passive homosexual, both with people of Rome and foreign hostages. 'Moreover,' writes Suetonius, 'a young man of consular family, Valerius Catullus, revealed publicly that he had buggered the Emperor, and quite worn himself out in the process.' He committed incest with his sisters, conducted an affair with a prostitute named Pyrallis, and made sexual advances to almost every respectable woman in Rome. His method of seduction was straightforward to say the least: he would invite a selection of women to dinner (with their husbands) and then, as each passed his couch, he would examine them at his leisure, 'as a purchaser might assess the value of a slave'. When he had decided on his favourite, Caligula would then leave the banquet with her, and would return later. As an added mortification to these unfortunate women (and as an added insult to the powerless husbands), he would describe in considerable detail not only their physical attributes, good and bad, but also their sexual performance. On certain occasions, he would even issue divorces in their husbands' names.

According to Suetonius, Caligula:

> practised many other various arts as well, most enthusiastically, too. He made appearances as a Thracian gladiator, as a singer, as a dancer, fought with real weapons, and drove chariots in many circuses in a number of places. Indeed, he was so proud of his voice and his dancing that he could not resist the temptation of supporting the tragic actors at public performances, and would repeat their gestures by way of praise or criticism.

It seems that on the very day of his assassination, Caligula ordered an all-night festival. He was very fond of dancing at night, and once summoned three senators to his palace at midnight. Trembling with terror (for they had no idea of the reason for their summoning), they were taken to a stage, onto which Caligula suddenly leaped, 'amid a tremendous racket of flutes'. Dressed in a cloak and ankle-length tunic, he performed a song and dance, and then just as suddenly jumped from the stage, leaving the befuddled senators to make their own way home.

The Senate was even more disillusioned with Caligula than the populace. Senators were treated with utter contempt by this madman with delusions of godhood; many were arbitrarily accused of treason and ordered to commit suicide. He had people tortured and executed while he ate dinner, and, had death not interrupted his plans, would have made his favourite horse a consul. The prospect of such a man occupying the throne of Rome for the foreseeable future was too much for the Senate, and a conspiracy to assassinate Caligula was set in motion. It succeeded in AD 41, when he was stabbed to death in his palace by a member of the Praetorian Guard.

COMMODUS

Commodus' character was equally dreadful, perhaps more so. His full name was Lucius Aelius Aurelius. One of the most notoriously perverted and decadent of ancient rulers, he was born in AD 161 at Lanuvium, the son of the Emperor Marcus Aurelius. Although good-natured as a child, he grew up to be one of the most awful and hated of Emperors. He became Emperor while in the army on the Danube. Instead of continuing to lead his men, he turned over the campaign against the Germans to his generals and returned to Rome, in order to take advantage of the fine weather, not to mention the numerous benefits that came with the Imperial throne.

His reign was characterised by mismanagement and, like Nero, he was far more inclined to pay attention to various sensual pursuits (with partners of both sexes) than to affairs of state. He frequently sold government offices to the highest bidder in order to swell his own coffers, and allowed Germanic tribes to push into the Empire on the condition that they lived peacefully there. This was seen as treason by the Senate, which turned against him and, with the help of Commodus' sister Lucilla, planned to assassinate him. When the attempt failed, the conspirators, including Lucilla, were executed.

Commodus was one of those Emperors who threw social graces to the winds and frequently appeared in the arena as a gladiator. In fact, he appeared more frequently than any other Emperor, at least one thousand times. He practised obsessively in his own home, and mastered the difficult art of left-handed fighting. Describing these domestic battles, Dio Cassius writes that 'Commodus managed to kill a man now and then, and in making close passes with others, as if trying to clip off a bit of their hair, he sliced off the noses of some, the ears of others, and sundry features of still others'. He took the greatest delight in causing pain and suffering to those around him.

Cruel as this was, it was as nothing compared to one occasion in the arena, in which Commodus performed the role of a Herculean hero. Once again, it is described by Dio Cassius:

> Once, he got together all the men in the city who had lost their feet as the result of disease or some accident, and then, after fastening about their knees some likenesses of serpents' bodies, and giving them sponges to throw instead of stones, killed them with blows of a club, pretending that they were giants.

Commodus had numerous animals brought into his palace, where he killed them one after another. He did the same with gladiators, practising upon them as upon wicker dummies. When he fought in the arena before the gathered spectators, he would take off his robes and put on a simple tunic, in which he fought as both gladiator and *bestiarius*. Each victory (which was really nothing of the kind, since his opponents invariably fought with wooden swords) elicited screams of delight from the plebeians and complimentary words from the senators and knights. Of course, to shout words of compliment to such a man was an act of self-preservation and nothing more. On some days, these words were even scripted and recited verbatim. One such paean went thus: 'You are the master, you are the first among us, you are the happiest of men. You are the victor, as you always will be, Amazonus, you are the victor.'

When 'fighting' against wild animals, Commodus had the arena divided into partitions to make his task easier still, and it was not unusual for him to kill a hundred bears single-handedly in one day. When he fought as a gladiator, Commodus occasionally gave the spectators the opportunity to choose his opponent. However, he insisted on receiving payment for his appearances in the arena and, needless to say, his fee was astronomical – as high as a million sesterces. He was extremely proud of his left-handedness (left-handed gladiators were particularly feared), and had this inscription carved on the plinth of the statue of himself: 'The *primus palus secutorum* who, being left-handed, vanquished twelve thousand men on his own, I believe.'

As might be expected of a man like Commodus, murderous jealousy was never far from his mind when he watched a gladiatorial combat or a *venatio*. On one occasion a *bestiarius* named Julius Alexander was pursuing a lion across the arena on horseback. Taking aim with his javelin, he let fly with it and killed the beast. This was a feat of considerable skill. So impressed was Commodus with the man's abilities that he immediately had him put to death.

Commodus made a great many enemies among his own people, as a result of his allowing soldiers to abuse and victimise civilians. He made even more enemies among his military governors by having their children 'cared for' in his custody; the children, in effect, were taken hostage to ensure the support of their parents, who were left in little doubt of the dreadful things that would be done to their little ones should they withdraw that support. His paranoia drove him to make a list of those he believed were plotting to assassinate him. This list included members of the Praetorian Guard, and when it was discovered, those on it decided that they had little to lose in actually assassinating him. Commodus was strangled to death by his bath attendant in AD 192.

CHAPTER ELEVEN

The Horror of
the Executions

XI

In the Roman arena, criminals tended to be executed at lunchtime, their agonising deaths forming a kind of macabre intermission between the hunts of the morning and the gladiatorial combats of the afternoon. The methods of execution reached truly mind-boggling extremes of cruelty. While it is generally believed that in the late Republic citizens who had been convicted of a serious crime were exiled rather than executed, those who did not enjoy citizen status could not expect any clemency whatsoever from public law. Up to the first century AD, the punishment meted out to slaves, for instance, was entirely up to their owners, and non-citizens such as the *dediticii* (members of conquered communities) were frequently liable to crucifixion. However, some cases of clemency (for various reasons) are on record, as with the Emperor Vitellius and his slave Asiaticus, reported by Suetonius:

Asiaticus had been Vitellius' slave and boy love, but soon grew tired of his role and ran away. After a while he was discovered selling cheap drinks at Puteoli, and put in chains until Vitellius ordered his release and made him his favourite again. However, Asiaticus behaved so insolently, and so thievishly as well, that Vitellius became irritated and sold him to an itinerant trainer of gladiators; but impulsively bought him back when he was just about to take part in the final match of a gladiatorial contest.

Vitellius lasted as Emperor for less than a year.

In addition, the governors of provinces could punish wrongdoers (not to mention those who had done no wrong) in any way they chose. Suetonius has an interesting – if frightful – anecdote concerning Galba, the governor in Spain:

> He sentenced a dishonest money-changer to have both hands cut off and nailed to the counter; and crucified a man who had poisoned his ward to inherit the property. When this murderer begged for justice, protesting that he was a Roman citizen, Galba recognised his status and ironically consoled him with: 'Let this citizen hang higher than the rest, and have his cross whitewashed.'

METHODS OF EXECUTION

There is some debate among historians as to whether methods of execution became more terrible as the centuries progressed. Wiedemann is not convinced, but notes that the number of offences for which the death penalty was prescribed certainly increased, and for two main reasons: first, that the Emperors wanted to be seen as being tough on criminals; and second, that by having the death penalty for a wide range of offences, they could commute it when they deemed it necessary, and thus appear to display compassionate virtue when the need arose. However, regulations 'ascribed to Hadrian by the *Historia Augusta* forbade masters from executing their slaves and insisted that they had to be condemned by state judges, and also that "Male or female slaves might not be sold to pimps or to trainers of gladiators unless due cause had been proved", implicitly before a court of law'.

After the *Constitutio Antoniniana* of AD 212, which granted citizenship to all free people throughout the Empire, the distinction implied by citizenship with regard to capital punishment ceased to have any relevance. Thus, a new distinction arose, between the *honestiores* (senators, soldiers, municipal council members, and so on) and the *humiliores* (everyone else). The punishment for the former was beheading by the sword, a method that was quick and relatively painless, assuming it was carried out by an executioner who knew his business. The *humiliores* could expect an altogether more protracted and painful end: some were crucified, some were burned to death (*ad flammas or crematio*), and some were torn limb from limb by wild animals (*ad bestias*).

To be sure, these punishments are truly awful (whatever one's views on the death penalty itself may be), since they aim to inflict the maximum pain possible on the individual. We cannot help but shrink from them in disgust. However, Wiedemann makes the essential point – and it is a point that must be applied to all of the gladiatorial spectacles – that to see the nature of Roman capital punishment as sadistic 'only makes sense in a culture where humanitarian sensibilities are taken as the norm'.

In ancient Rome, however, the infliction of pain was an essential part of punishment. The Emperor Constantine (who ruled from AD 306–37), for instance, decided that those involved in the abduction of a virgin should have molten lead poured down their throats. However, strictly speaking we are not really justified in calling the infliction of pain 'sadistic', at least in the Roman context, since it was not inflicted for its own sake, but rather as a corollary to the level of suffering caused by the criminal's activities. For instance, a man convicted of arson could expect to be burned alive; one guilty of fraud would have his hands amputated. The infliction of physical pain was also important as a tool of humiliation. The person who commits a crime assumes certain rights to which he has no true claim (for instance, the right to take another's property). His actions, therefore, upset the balanced functioning of society with its various status levels. The infliction of pain and humiliation thus cancel out the spurious rights the criminal originally claimed for himself. In addition, the deterrent value of such punishments was of great importance, and resulted in crucified criminals being displayed in those places most frequented by the populace, so that as many people as possible might see the fate of the wrongdoer, and be warned by it.

These extremes of punishment were justified by Seneca thus:

> The law has three aims in punishing injuries (and the Emperor should have the same three aims): either to reform the person being punished, or to make others behave better as a result of his punishment, or so that the rest of us can lead our lives more securely with evil-doers eliminated.

At Rome, the throwing of criminals to wild beasts tended to form just one part of the *venatio*, which began in the morning, and extended into the lunchtime period of executions. In the provinces, however, executions *ad bestias* sometimes went on for an entire day. This happened in Lyons in AD 177, where 48 sentences were carried out. On this occasion, the condemned were Christians who were known to the public, and so the spectators shouted for them by name. At Rome, it was unusual for the crowd to know the names of the people whose deaths it was watching. Indeed, this only really happened when some particularly notorious brigand was being despatched, or when the crime had been an unusual or titillating one, as with the tutor of Glyco in Petronius' *Satyricon*:

> He's got some real desperadoes already, and a woman who fights in a chariot, and Glyco's steward who was caught having fun with his mistress. You'll see quite a quarrel in the crowd between jealous husbands and romantic lovers. But that half-pint Glyco threw his steward to the lions, which is just giving himself away. How is it the servant's fault when

he's forced into it? It's that old pisspot who really deserves to be tossed by a bull.

THE PUNISHMENT OF SLAVES

One type of criminal was particularly feared in ancient Rome – the criminal slave, the enemy within who might steal from or even murder his master. The punishment of slaves was the responsibility of their owner, and this was another reason for the punishments being performed in public: so that the rest of society could see that the slaves were being punished as they deserved. Although it was hardly in an owner's interest to have his slave treated unnecessarily severely (thus damaging a valuable piece of property), slaves were routinely executed. Since few people had the means to carry out the executions themselves, municipal executioners were provided, and the manner of the execution itself was regulated by the civic authorities. Thus, we read in a first-century AD inscription from Puteoli:

> If anyone wishes to have a slave – male or female – punished privately, he who wishes to have the punishment inflicted shall do so as follows. If he wants to put the slave on the cross or fork [i.e. crucify him], the contractor must supply the posts, chains, ropes for floggers and the floggers themselves. The person having the punishment inflicted is to pay 4 sesterces for each of the operatives who carry the fork, and the same for the floggers and for the executioner.
>
> The magistrate shall give orders for such punishments as he exacts in his public capacity, and when orders are given, the contractor is to be ready to exact the punishment. He is to set up crosses and supply without charge nails, pitch, wax, tapers and anything else that is necessary for this in order to deal with the condemned man. Again, if he is ordered to drag away the corpse with a hook, the work-gang is to be dressed

in red and ring a bell while dragging away the body, or bodies if there are several.

If a commission is given to remove a hanged man, he (the contractor) is to see to its fulfilment and the removal (of the body) within the hour. If it is for a male or female slave, if the notification is received before the tenth hour, removal is to be effected the same day; if after the tenth hour, then before the second hour on the following day.

ABANDONED TO THE CARNIVORES

The practise of throwing people to wild beasts probably originated in Carthage, and was initially the fate of foreign deserters from Roman armies. It was the most shameful of all punishments (as befitted army deserters), and was later used against slaves and Christians. The condemned were called *bestiarii*, the same word as used to denote the professional gladiators who specialised in hunting and killing wild animals in the arena.

The condemned criminal would be separated from his fellows (they were all initially chained together at the neck) and stripped of his clothes. If his crime was particularly hateful, for example if he was a Christian, he would be forced to make a tour of the arena, a sort of inverted victory lap, with a tablet bearing his name and 'the Christian'. Most often, however, the crime was written upon the *stipes*, the column of shame. To this column the condemned would be tied with his hands behind his back. And then the beasts, having been trained to eat men – and starved, for good measure – were released into the arena to wreak havoc on the hapless criminal.

Dangerous carnivores were imported from all over the Empire, and it was a lucky *bestiarius* who was knocked mercifully unconscious by the paw of a big cat, or else killed instantly by the snap of powerful jaws. As Auguet comments, they were 'less cruel executioners than some of the smaller beasts which dragged and tore their quivering victims in protracted torture; in Martial's expression, the victim no longer "had the semblance of a body" and it was necessary finally to kill him off . . .'

Astonishingly, the statues surrounding the arena were covered with veils so that they would be spared the view of spraying blood and bursting organs, a sight which the Emperor Claudius did not find in the least disturbing: he frequently had dinner while watching the carnage, although he did at least have the decency to move the statue of Augustus, so that it would not have to be continually covered!

CRUELTY AND RESTRAINT

Claudius I (10 BC – AD 54), whose full name was Tiberius Claudius Drusus Nero Germanicus was Emperor from AD 41 to 54. He was born in Lugdunum (present-day Lyon, France). His inability to control his limbs properly, coupled with the severe difficulties he experienced when speaking in public, has led historians to suggest that Claudius may have been born with cerebral palsy. His illustrious family background notwithstanding – his father, Nero Claudius Drusus, was a younger brother of Tiberius Claudius Nero Caesar (later the Emperor Tiberius) – Claudius held no important office until he was 47, when he became consul under his infamous nephew, Emperor Caligula.

When Caligula was assassinated in AD 41, Claudius was discovered by the Praetorian Guard cowering behind a curtain in the Imperial palace. He rewarded the Guard with money, a wise act, which went a considerable way towards securing the throne for him. Although his early reign was clement and just, a conspiracy against his life in 42 prompted him to enter semi-retirement, leaving his third wife, Messalina (c. 22–48) in charge of government administration. Messalina was an extremely promiscuous sexual predator, and manipulated Claudius into executing a number of men who had either rejected her advances, or had angered her in some way. Traditionally, historians have seen her as a selfish, immature nymphomaniac who spent a good deal of her time holding wild, orgiastic parties; however, there have been some attempts by scholars to rehabilitate her, portraying her as an astute player of the political game (no easy feat for a woman in ancient Rome), who skilfully used sex as a weapon.

While Claudius was away in Ostia in AD 48, Messalina held a party in the palace, during which she took part in a (perhaps mock) marriage ceremony with a young senator named Gaius Silius. Whatever the true purpose of this, it could not fail to be seen as an attempt to overthrow Claudius and place Silius on the throne. As a result, Messalina and Silius were summarily executed. In spite of Messalina's influence, Claudius' reign was characterised by good administration. The conquest of Britain was begun, and Rome's armies secured victories against the Germans. Judea and Thrace also became Roman provinces under Claudius' rule.

Following Messalina's execution, Claudius married his niece, Agrippina the Younger, despite widespread disapproval. It was under her influence that Claudius deprived Britannicus (his son by Messalina) of his heritage, in favour of Nero, Agrippina's son by an earlier marriage.

Suetonius has much to say on the humanity (or lack thereof) of Claudius:

> His cruelty and bloodthirstiness appeared equally in great and small matters. For instance, if evidence had to be extracted under torture, or parricide punished, he allowed the Law to take its course without delay and in his own presence. Once, when an old-fashioned execution had been ordered at Tibur and the criminals had been tied to their stakes, no executioner

could be found to carry it out; but Claudius summoned one from Rome and was so set on witnessing the procedure that he waited until dusk for the man's arrival. At gladiatorial shows, whether or not they were staged by himself, he ruled that all combatants who fell accidentally should have their throats cut – above all net-fighters, so that he could gaze on their death agony. When a pair of gladiators mortally wounded each other he sent for their swords and had pocket-knives made from them for his personal use. Claudius so greatly enjoyed wild-beast shows and the fencing matches during the luncheon interval that, after he had spent the whole morning in the amphitheatre from daybreak until noon, he would dismiss the audience, keep his seat, and not only watch the regular combats but extemporise others between the stage carpenters, and similar members of the theatre staff, as a punishment for the failure of any mechanical device to work as it should. He even forced one of his pages to enter the arena just as he was, and fight in his toga.

Not all Emperors were quite this bloodthirsty, and the classical literature holds many examples of surprising clemency. For instance, Suetonius tells how Julius Caesar decided against torturing a traitorous slave before killing him. 'When his secretary, the slave Philemon, promised his enemies to kill him by poison, he punished him by nothing more severe than a straightforward execution.'

Augustus also could show great restraint. This also from Suetonius:

When a slave called Cosmus made serious accusations against him [Augustus], his punishment went no further than shackling. When he went for a walk with his steward Diomedes and a wild boar suddenly attacked them, Diomedes left him in the lurch; but Augustus preferred to accuse him of cowardice than of a crime, and he made fun of an incident that was extremely serious, since the slave had meant no harm. But he also forced one of his favourite freedmen, Polus, to commit suicide when he was discovered to have been seducing married women; he broke the legs of his secretary Thallus for having betrayed the contents of a letter for 500 *denarii*; and he had the *paedagogi* and servants of his [adopted] son Gaius thrown into the river with heavy weights tied to their necks because of the insolence and greed with which they had behaved out in [Asia] at the time when Gaius was sick and dying.

ANDROCLES AND THE LION

Very occasionally, some unusual event would occur in the arena to break the monotony of ripped corpses, and these would give rise to various legends, the most famous of which is, of course, that of Androcles and the lion. Many readers will doubtless be familiar with this rather charming tale learnt in their school days. Briefly, the legend tells of how a Dacian slave was faced with a ferocious lion, which nevertheless refused to attack him, and instead licked his feet. When a leopard was sent into the arena, the lion turned on it and killed it. The *editor* of the games, Drusus, had the slave brought before him and demanded to know why the lion had refused to attack him. Androcles replied that he had fled from his master, the proconsul for Africa, and had hid in a desert cave. A lion had appeared, with a thorn in its paw. Androcles removed it, and the grateful lion became his servant, bringing freshly killed meat to the cave while the slave continued to hide from the soldiers despatched to search for him. Eventually, Androcles grew tired of his rather basic diet, ventured outside and was recaptured. His master condemned him *ad bestias*. The legend ends with both Androcles and the lion being granted their freedom.

PERSECUTION OF THE CHRISTIANS

During the Empire, the state implemented tight controls on the degree of punishment a master might inflict upon his slave, not so much from humanitarianism as from a desire to reserve the power to take life for itself rather than the citizenry. Although slaves continued to be executed, this could only be done with the approval of a public court, as opposed to the family council, which had hitherto sat in judgement of errant slaves. Allied to this was the decision to restrict public executions to particular times (the games), and to one particular place (Rome). From the first century AD, criminals were sent to Rome from all over the Empire to face the beasts or the flames. It was thus logical to limit the venue of execution largely to the amphitheatre, since this was the place where the wild animals could be kept with the greatest degree of security.

Of course, the most famous victims of Roman executions were the Christians, and it is certainly true that we can learn a great deal about the subject from the experiences of Christians who were executed for no crime other than their religion. In his *Epistle to the Romans*, St Ignatius of Antioch provides a chilling account:

> I have already been finding myself in conflict with beasts of prey by land and by sea, by night and by day, the whole way from Syria to Rome: chained as I am to half-a-score of savage leopards [by which he means a detachment of soldiers], who only grow more insolent the more bribes they are given . . . How I look forward to the real lions that have been prepared for me! All I pray is that I will find them swift. I am going to make overtures to them, so that, unlike some other wretches whom they have been too spiritless to touch, they will devour me with all speed. And if they are reluctant, I shall have to use force on them . . . Fire, cross, beast-fighting, hacking and

quartering, splintering of bone and mangling of limb, even the pulverising of my whole body – let every horrid and diabolical torment come upon me, provided only that I can win my way to Jesus Christ!

The Christian Bishop Polycarp of Smyrna was burnt to death in the Circus at Smyrna around AD 155; others of his community were condemned to the beasts. Eyewitness accounts of this time offer further awful details of what had to be endured before merciful death found them. Polycarp was taken before the Governor of Smyrna and given the opportunity to renounce Christianity and make a sacrifice to Caesar:

> The governor then said, 'I have wild beasts here. Unless you change your mind, I shall have you thrown to them.'
>
> 'Why then, call them up,' said Polycarp, 'for it is out of the question for us to exchange a proper faith for a bad one. It would be a very creditable thing, though, to change over from the wrong to the right.'
>
> The other said again, 'If you do not recant, I will have you burnt to death, since you think so lightly of wild beasts.'
>
> Polycarp replied: 'The fire you threaten me with cannot go on burning for very long: after a while it goes out. But what you are unaware of is the flames of future judgement and everlasting torment which are in store for the ungodly. Why do you go on wasting time? Bring out whatever you have a mind to.'

The crowd assembled in the Circus demanded that Polycarp be given to a lion; however, the annual games had been declared closed, and so to condemn a man *ad bestias* would have been illegal. When informed of this, the people cried for Polycarp to be burned alive:

There he was in the centre of it, not like a human being in flames but like a loaf baking in the oven, or like a gold or silver ingot being refined in the furnace. And we became aware of a delicious fragrance, like the odour of incense or other precious gums.

This delightful smell was nothing like the nauseating stench normally associated with burning human flesh. It seemed that the body of Polycarp could not be destroyed by fire. This did not deter his tormentors, however: they simply stabbed him to death instead.

In truth, the cruelty of Roman executions knew no bounds. One of the best known is Nero's treatment of the Christians whom he blamed for starting the Great Fire at Rome in AD 64.

CRUELTY AND DEBAUCHERY

Nero (AD 37–68), whose full name was Nero Claudius Caesar Drusus Germanicus, was the fifth Emperor of Rome and the last of the Julio-Claudian line. Born at Antium, and originally named Lucius Domitius Ahenobarbus, he was the son of the consul Gnaeus Domitius Ahenobarbus and Agrippina the Younger, the great-granddaughter of the Emperor Augustus. Agrippina married her uncle, Emperor Claudius, and persuaded him to adopt her son Lucius, whose name was changed.

Claudius married Nero to his daughter Octavia, and named him as his successor instead of his own son, Britannicus. On Claudius' death in 54, the Praetorian Guards declared Nero Emperor. He was 17.

Although there was the occasional aberration, such as the poisoning of his rival Britannicus, for the first five years of his reign Nero was a generous and moderate Emperor (in stark contrast to later years), and was guided by the philosopher Seneca and Sextus Afranius Burrus, the Prefect of the

Praetorian Guards. However, in 59, when his mother, who had exercised considerable influence over his reign, criticised his mistress, Poppaea Sabina, Nero had her executed. Three years later, he divorced and executed Octavia, and married Poppaea.

Nero was a vicious, self-indulgent, vacuous nonentity, whose assertion early in his reign that he would emulate his great ancestor, Augustus, was never fulfilled. In fact, as Michael Grant notes in his biography of the Emperor, he shared far more in common with the sado-masochistic Tiberius and the utterly deranged Caligula. His nights were spent indulging in sexual debauchery, and his days in chariot racing, acting and singing on the stage (activities that were incredibly unseemly for an Emperor). He worked very hard to develop his singing voice, following the usual procedures, such as lying on his back with a lead weight on his chest, and using enemas to keep his weight down. Vegetables of the onion family were believed to be good for the voice, and so Nero added these to his diet. As Grant wryly comments: 'It is good to know after this (and after Suetonius' report that he suffered from body odour as well) that the Emperor scented not only his bath water, but his hands and the soles of his feet.'

Nero was also fond of prowling through the streets of Rome at night, drinking heavily, picking fights with people and having his way with women and boys. One evening, Nero picked on a senator named Montanus. When he punched him, Montanus punched back, and then apologised. This, it turned out, was a fatal mistake, because it alerted Nero to the fact that Montanus knew who he was. As a result, Montanus was forced to commit suicide, and from then on, Nero took guardsmen and gladiators with him whenever he went carousing through the night-time streets of the city. Thus, whenever Nero started a fight, his bully-boys could be counted on to finish it.

Tacitus has this to say on Nero's night-time excursions:

In the theatre, there were brawls between gangs favouring rival ballet-dancers. Nero converted these disorders into serious warfare. For he waived penalties and offered prizes – watching in person, secretly and on many occasions even openly. Finally, however, public animosities and fears of worse disturbances left no alternative but to expel these dancers from Italy and station troops in the theatre again.

Nero also had a particularly voracious sexual appetite, and admired this trait in others. According to Suetonius, 'it was Nero's own unshaken conviction that no man was chaste or pure in any part of his body, but that most of them concealed their vices and cleverly drew a veil over them; and that therefore he pardoned all other faults in those who confessed to him their obscene practices.' This attitude was fashionable in Rome at the time; in fact, Neronian society was permissive in a way that would put the late 1960s to shame. It was also common to speculate wildly about the private lives of those in the imperial court, and Nero's sexual affairs were no exception. It was said, for instance, that he took no sexual interest in his wife Octavia, but frequently went to bed with his mother. He also enjoyed sex with men and boys, both slaves and free-born citizens.

On one occasion, he was said to have gone through a marriage ceremony with one of his ministers, a Greek named Doryphorus. In the words of Tacitus: 'In the presence of witnesses, Nero put on the bridal veil! Dowry, marriage bed, wedding torches, all were there. Indeed everything was public which, even at a natural union, is veiled by night.' On his 'wedding night', he also screamed and moaned like a chaste bride losing her virginity. According to Suetonius, Nero also played an extremely perverse game in which he dressed himself in animal skins and had himself locked in a cage. He would then be released, and would run at various men and women who had been tied, naked, to stakes. In this animal guise, he would then perform oral sex upon them.

The Great Fire of Rome, perhaps the event with which Nero is most identified, occurred in the summer of 64. Nero was at Antium when the fire started in the *Circus Maximus*. It burned for nine days, and destroyed two thirds of the city. Upon his return, Nero immediately set about rebuilding the city, and rumours started to circulate that he had been responsible for the fire, with the intention of clearing land for the construction of his vast and opulent palace, the Golden House. It is, however, extremely unlikely that Nero was responsible for the great fire: for one thing, it started a long way from the area he had in mind for his palace, and actually destroyed another of his palaces on the Palatine.

In order to divert public attention from these rumours, Nero and his advisors placed the blame for the fire on the most unpopular and vulnerable group of the time: the Christians. It is unlikely that Nero really believed that the Christians were to blame, but they made a perfect scapegoat, and were made to suffer dreadfully for their 'crime'. According to Tacitus:

> First, Nero had self-acknowledged Christians arrested. Then, on their information, large numbers of others were condemned – not so much for incendiarism as for their anti-social tendencies. Their deaths were made farcical. Dressed in wild animals' skins, they were torn to pieces by dogs, or crucified, or made into torches to be ignited after dark as substitutes for daylight. Nero provided his Gardens for the spectacle, and exhibited displays in the Circus, at which he mingled with the crowd – or stood in a chariot, dressed as a charioteer.

Nero's tyrannical attitude and political and military incompetence resulted in the Pisonian Conspiracy, in which a group of senators planned to assassinate him and replace him with

Calpurnius Piso. When the conspirators were discovered, they also suffered terrible fates; Seneca and his nephew, the epic poet Lucan, were among the victims. Poppaea died when Nero kicked her during an argument (it seems that he did not mean to kill her). Nero then married Statilia Messalina after executing her husband.

In 68, the Gallic and Spanish legions and the Praetorian Guards rose against him, and he fled Rome. Declared a public enemy by the Senate, he took his own life the same year.

STRANGE DRAMAS

The tasks assigned to the condemned while in the arena were dreadfully cruel and inventive; for instance, a bull and a bear would be chained together in the arena, and an unarmed *bestiarius* would be persuaded with whip and branding-iron to use a long hook to detach the chains linking them. The bull and bear would fight viciously while chained, but once separated, they would almost invariably turn their attention to the hapless criminal. Others would be tied to stakes, or even wheeled into the arena in little carts, and abandoned to the animals. Alternatively, criminals would be forced to fight each other with swords, but no armour. The victor would have to face a new opponent (also a convicted criminal) time and again until he himself was killed, and so on. In this way, the condemned were forced to execute each other. All in all, the *venatio* was a chilling combination of entertainment and justice, and escape was virtually impossible. Seneca, however, tells us of one man who was able to cheat the crowd of their spectacle:

A German who was slated to be one of the wild animal fighters in the arena was getting ready for the morning show. He withdrew to relieve himself – the only thing he was allowed to do on his own without a guard being present. In the toilet there was a stick with a sponge on the end of it used for wiping away the faeces. He rammed the whole thing down his throat and choked to death . . . Not a very elegant way to go, it's true, but what is more foolish than to be overly fastidious about our departure? What a brave man!

It is something of an ambivalent tribute to the elaborate Roman imagination that straightforward executions in the arena, by fire or beast, were not quite interesting enough. Added to them were the dramas in which convicted criminals were forced to participate as characters from Greco-Roman mythology, and which served as frameworks for the hideous manner of their executions.

From the time of Nero onwards, Emperors had criminals executed in the course of dramatic performances. Traditional mimes were also utilised for this purpose. In the *Book of Spectacles*, attributed to the poet Martial, we find the following description of a public execution in which the condemned criminal is forced to play the traditional part of the chieftain Laureolus:

Just as Prometheus provided the unremitting vulture with food when he was chained to that rock in Scythia, so Laureolus offered his entrails to a Caledonian bear as he hung from a cross which was no stage-prop. Dripping with blood, his torn limbs continued to live, and there was no substance left in any part of his body.

In the end he suffered the punishment he deserved: the criminal had cut the throat of parent or master with a sword, or had plundered a temple of the gold entrusted to it, or had savagely set fire to you, Rome. His crime had exceeded those of ancient stories; what had been a play became this man's punishment.

There is some debate among historians as to the meaning of these displays, in which real criminals were killed in the death scenes of mimes and plays. It was during the Empire that these demonstrations took place. Some suggest that it was merely to make these scenes more realistic, while others maintain the very opposite: that it reflects a lack of reality with regard to public life, which professed the continuance of liberty (as was the case during the Republic), but which was actually far from the case under the Empire. Interestingly, each of these viewpoints can be supported with regard to the meticulous detail in which the scenes of the executions were created. On these occasions, the arena was transformed with great technical skill into forests and clearings, using real grass and trees. Again, this can be seen as a way of making the drama more 'real', but also as a way of reinforcing an illusion which has its corollary in the difference between Republican liberty and Imperial power. Wiedemann suggests another, 'less sophisticated' reason: the need to hold the attention of a notoriously fickle public. As we have already seen, nothing held the interest of the public more successfully than an interesting innovation.

The first reference to an execution conducted within the context of a myth comes from Nero's reign, and concerns a thief named Meniscus who, it seems, stole three apples from Nero's Golden House. The poet Lucillius tells of how this thief's punishment was to be wrapped in a tunic smeared with pitch (*tunica molesta*) and then set alight. Lucillius compares this fate with that of Herakles, who was given a coat smeared with the blood of the centaur Nessus by his wife Deianeira. When he put on the coat, it burnt him to death.

On many occasions, the manner of execution took considerable liberties with the myths they were supposed to represent. Two examples in particular stand out. In the first, a criminal who had been condemned to play the part of Orpheus would be chained to a rock in the arena. A number of tamed animals would enter, giving the impression of being charmed by the music from 'Orpheus'' lyre. A wild bear would then enter and, instead of being charmed, would immediately rip him to shreds. The second example concerns the myth of Daedalus. The condemned criminal would be given a set of artificial wings, and would be suspended above the arena by strings. In this drama, the hapless 'Daedalus' does not reach his destination, but is dropped to the ground, where a bear puts a bloody end to him.

Under Nero this practice reached a nadir of atrocity with the enactment of the myth of Pasiphae, who as a result of intercourse with a white bull gave birth to the Minotaur. On these occasions, a condemned woman would be imprisoned inside a wooden heifer and a rampant bull allowed into the arena. What followed is perhaps best left to the reader's imagination.

Having examined the lives of gladiators and their place within Roman society, let us now travel back through time to a certain day during the reign of Commodus. The chapter that follows is merely invention in terms of the many incidents it describes, and yet they are all incidents which might well have happened on that day in ancient Rome. The purpose of the chapter is to provide the reader with a taste of what it might have been like to tread the streets of the capital and take a seat in the Flavian Amphitheatre on that day.

CHAPTER TWELVE

A Day at the Games

XII

A DESPERATE ESCAPE

The cart jolted suddenly, shaking the slave out of his exhausted sleep. Dawn was breaking, and with his return to wakefulness came the recollection, instant and dreadful, that this day was to be his last on Earth. The slave's name was Attalus. As he watched the countryside move past, its tranquillity broken only by the clatter of the cart's wheels on the dry earth of the highway, he thought again (perhaps for the hundredth time) of what had happened to bring him to this place, on this day.

Attalus' master had been a harsh and vindictive one – dreadfully so. Not only had he beaten and flogged him at every opportunity, for the most trivial of misdemeanours, but had also taken the greatest delight in telling him that one day he would be made to die in the arena, no matter how obedient he strove to be, now matter how convincingly he proclaimed his love for his master even as the whip shredded his flesh. It was his master's pleasure to make it clear to Attalus that he was to live a life of pain and anguish, for no other reason than that the master willed it to be so, and that he would ensure that his life ended under the pitiless heat of the midday sun, with the lustful roar of 50,000 spectators pounding in his ears.

Attalus endured this for many years, for he knew well what happened to slaves with whom their masters grew sufficiently displeased. The very best they could hope for would be to be sold into a *familia gladiatoria*, where the beatings and misery would continue until they had been trained sufficiently to fight in the arena. Of the many ways for a slave to die, this was the most bearable: a single sword thrust to the neck, a gout of blood, and merciful oblivion. For the others, the agonies in store were revolting. The *tunica molesta*, the tunic covered with pitch, a burning torch promising the unendurable: a screaming death as one's flesh was destroyed by fire. Or punishment *ad bestias*: cast into the arena to face the wild carnivores, armed with nothing but the desire for a swift end. Or crucifixion, hung like a putrefying carcass upon a cross, until the muscles in one's neck weakened, the head sank forward onto the chest, gradually closing off the windpipe and causing slow suffocation.

Images such as these had haunted Attalus' sleep, chased through his restless mind by the words proclaiming a destiny only his master controlled. Every day became a tightrope walk over the abyss, in which the slightest mistake could herald the plunge into the unbearable.

And then came the evening, a week earlier, when the crowning misery had descended upon him. A moment's carelessness, and a goblet lay smashed on the floor. The fury that arose in his master's eyes – a fury laced with savage glee at the punishment to come – had made Attalus want to run from the villa, to dash headlong with the greatest speed he could muster, out into the twilight, to be anywhere . . . anywhere but here. But instead, the blows rained upon him, the whip flicked his flesh, each touch like that of lightning. Even in his terror, he wondered how a mere instant of contact could cause the flowering of such awful pain.

When Attalus thought he could bear no more, his master suddenly stopped in mid-stroke. They were both panting, both glistening with sweat. For a moment, Attalus thought that the punishment was over, but when, against his better judgement, he risked a glance at his master's face, he saw in it something bestial, something inhuman. An idea had occurred to him, delicious in its awfulness, by which he might increase his slave's misery and contrition a hundredfold. The master let his toga drop to the floor, and Attalus closed his eyes tight as the ultimate humiliation began.

The following day, Attalus fled from his master's house, the memory of the atrocity committed upon him burning in his mind. The frightfulness of the attack, combined with the knowledge that this new method of punishment had appealed greatly to his master and would almost certainly be repeated whenever the whim took him, had left Attalus no choice but to attempt an escape, with all the dire consequences that implied.

Although the villa was no more than a distant white glint in the morning sunlight, Attalus nevertheless thought he could feel his master's eyes still upon him, glowing with feral passion, bathed in a miasma of lust that went far beyond that of the flesh. It was his master's lust for control that had been sated the previous night. It was not just from physical harm that Attalus had fled that morning; it was from the necessity of looking into those eyes every day for the rest of his life.

Of course, the escape had not been planned. It was a wild, panic-driven flight without thought for how his sudden freedom could be prolonged, and by midday, Attalus had been recaptured. Whether through boredom with the new torment he had devised, or through a sudden desire to make good his threats as quickly as possible, Attalus' master merely locked him away in his quarters while he made arrangements for the slave to be taken from his house to the arena.

Now Attalus' thoughts returned to the rattling, jolting cart making its way through the tranquil countryside to the very antithesis of tranquillity. He regarded his fellows, three other slaves slung into the cart by their masters for unknown crimes – perhaps for no crimes at all. The same fate, to meet death in the arena, awaited them all; only the manner of its descending upon them had yet to be determined.

As they approached the city, Attalus' fear grew. He could scarcely imagine the agonies that were in store for him, and with each passing moment, his muscles grew more taught, his breathing more strained, his eyes wilder. The shackle about his neck, tying him to the other slaves by means of a long chain, seemed to constrict like a hungry python, squeezing the life out of its victim. If only that were true, he thought; if only the shackle, through some merciful miracle, could close suddenly upon his throat, putting a quick end to him, then and there. His desperation increasing as they drew nearer to the city, Attalus thought again and again: 'If only I could die now. If only I could find a way to escape . . . to escape once and for all time . . .'

In utter despair, he raised his eyes to the deep azure sky, and then slowly lay down flat on the floor of the cart. A few wispy clouds hung high in the air, their tendrils moving too slowly to be perceptible. Indeed, from this position the only movement of which Attalus was aware was that of the cart's wheels, the upper part of which he could see spinning with cruel relentlessness.

It was then that the thought occurred to him, an idea both terrible and beautiful; terrible in its nature, yet beautiful in what it would achieve. Slowly, painfully, he raised himself to a sitting position, from which he regarded the upper section of the wheel nearest to him. He realised that in the spinning wooden arc lay his salvation, his way of escape from the looming amphitheatre. It would, he knew, be a vile death, but a swift one – perhaps too swift even to allow any pain.

With terrible certainty, Attalus realised that this was his last chance: the cart was already slowing, soon he would be dragged from it with the other slaves and taken into a realm of unthinkable agonies. He would have to act quickly, a moment's courage and all would be at an end. His master would be cheated of the satisfaction of watching Attalus' death. His woes would be vanquished. A moment's courage . . .

Raising himself to his knees, Attalus regarded the spinning cartwheel, breathing deeply, as if the very air contained the fortitude necessary for this final act. With his left hand, he dragged the chain connecting him to the next slave towards him a little, just enough to ensure him the degree of movement he would require.

The time to act was upon him. The interval between the thought and the deed could not have encompassed more than thirty beats of his frantic heart. The courage was his; the power to alter his own destiny nestled in the damp palms of his hands as they gripped the side of the cart. With a single motion, Attalus raised himself to his feet, closed his eyes and thrust his head into the whirling spokes of the wheel.

A moment's courage, a moment's pain, and it was done. Attalus' neck snapped in an instant. His head, caught between the spokes, shattered several of them and was wrenched sideways and torn almost completely from his shoulders, releasing a glistening, crimson shower. The cart driver glanced over his shoulder, saw what had happened and brought the vehicle to a sudden stop, the horse whinnying and snorting in protest.

The surviving slaves sat transfixed as the driver inspected the wrecked body, and the damage it had done to his cart. He gazed once more at Attalus' ruined head, and cursed him for this inconvenience. The condemned slave was beyond his fulminations, beyond the terror and pain of this world, beyond fire, tooth and claw. The remaining slaves looked at Attalus' inert body, and envied him.

THE SPECTATORS ARRIVE

From the previous day, Rome had swelled with Italians and foreigners who had come from all parts. Placards set up along the main roads, on tombs and verges, had advertised the staging of a spectacle, and had attracted people from across the social spectrum. From the rich in their country villas to the meanest peasants, all had come to the city in expectation of a fine day of games. On a day like this, Rome could not accommodate the extra thousands who flocked there, and so a myriad tents sprang up in the streets, giving the impression more of some dreadful natural disaster than of an activity that was entirely normal and awaited by the chattering people with excited anticipation.

On this day, while the cart driver was dragging Attalus' broken body from his damaged vehicle, the streets of Rome were in the process of emptying as the multitude made their way to the Flavian Amphitheatre. Philosophers stood by and watched with mild contempt as the plebeian throng moved past. For them, Rome would become as peaceful as a cemetery, the silence broken only by the occasional distant roar or clatter of applause from the amphitheatre, and they would be able to stroll through the empty streets in perfect tranquillity, at one with their thoughts. Other eyes watched the passers-by in less noble meditation. A day spent at the games meant an empty house, a fact not lost on the many thieves and villainous ne'er-do-wells who stalked the city.

The people entered the amphitheatre in their thousands by means of steep staircases, which led to a series of covered walkways known as *ambulacra*, leading in turn to the interior of the gigantic building. They then made their way through the *vomitoria*, the openings that gave access to the various seating areas.

Anyone standing in the empty amphitheatre would have had little clue as to the demarcations of Roman society that were embodied there. It was only as the place was filling up that they would become apparent from the white togas, which extended about two thirds of the way up the cavea, the interior of the building where all spectators sat, and the dark clothes of the poorer people that filled the remainder of the space. The cavea itself was divided into four ring-like sections by three walls (*baltei*); the highest section was further subdivided, so that the cavea contained five sections in all.

The first section, called the *podium* contained four tiers of seats and was immediately above the arena. It contained the Emperor's box, which was situated on the lesser axis of the arena, near the entrance. Opposite the Emperor's box stood another box reserved for the consuls. Visiting dignitaries also sat here. History shows that it was not always a good idea for such dignitaries to draw attention to themselves on these occasions. When a King of Egypt attended the games during Caligula's reign, and enlivened his dress with a bright purple mantle, thus causing something of a stir among the spectators, Caligula promptly ordered his execution.

The *podium* was bounded above and below by a wall: the lower, or front wall, was thirteen feet high, made of marble, and descended to the arena floor; the upper wall (the first *balteus*) was decorated with mosaics. The senators, magistrates and vestals now entered the *podium*, which was wider than the other parts of the cavea since it contained the chairs to be used by these illustrious persons.

The knights, tribunes and citizens then took their places directly above the podium in the first and second *maenianum*, which contained two ranks of tiers separated by the second *balteus*. The heat and humidity was such that they had already begun to sweat, and they wiped the greasy moisture from their expectant faces with plum, jewel-encrusted fingers. The last *balteus*, between the second and third *maenianum*, effectively provided the boundary of that part of the amphitheatre in which the patricians comfortably sat. Behind this were the sections where non-citizens were allowed to sit, along with the slaves and women. These presented a pretty wretched sight as they scrambled to their seats, their clothes and shoes ragged and in dire need of repair.

The massive crowd slowly moved through the corridors (*praecinctiones*) encircling the arena, and up the staircases (*scalaria*) which extended from the doors in the third *balteus* down to the *podium*. Those who had already found their seats watched the newest arrivals avidly, and gossiped among themselves, exchanging scandalous titbits concerning this or that illustrious personage. Others consulted the *libellus numerarius*, bought earlier from vendors in the streets; these were programme listing the names of the gladiators they were to see that day. Loudly and animatedly, they discussed their various chances of survival.

Each member of the audience held a counter designating the place at which he was to sit. One such counter, for example, read: *Cun VI Inferiori gradu decimo VIII*. This meant: Cuneus 6 (one of the wedge-like areas enclosed between the vertical staircases), lower tier number 10, place number 8.

The last to arrive were usually prominent politicians and other personalities, who might receive rapturous applause or shouted abuse from the onlookers, depending on the favour in which they were held at that particular time. When the Emperor himself appeared, all applauded and stood to greet him.

When everyone had seated themselves, they saw with satisfaction and anticipation that the spectacles were about to begin. The first attractions were the animals, the *venatio*.

THE MORNING HUNT

Although the hunts had begun many years before as a mere preamble to the gladiatorial combats in the afternoon, they had quickly grown in popularity with the easily-jaded Romans. By the end of the Republic, they had become at least as popular as the *munera* proper, and the crowd was always ready to gape in wonder at some new and exotic beast, dragged from its home to die here in Rome, at the heart of the greatest empire the world had ever known.

The animals, then, would be forced to battle each other. Teams of *magistri*, dressed in tunics and with no weapons other than clumps of burning straw, watched in ill-disguised trepidation the movements within the dark cubicles set into the *podium* surrounding the arena. A sudden hush fell upon the spectators as two of the cage doors were raised. When the bear and bull entered the arena, the crowd exploded once again with shouts and cheering.

The bear, eight feet of fur and muscle, regarded its new surroundings in shock: the vast expanse of empty sand, the thousands of screaming creatures surrounding it, must have presented a terrifying sight to the unfortunate creature. When it saw the bull on the far side of the arena, however, surprise gave way to instinctive fury. Here was something the bear could understand, a powerful and dangerous enemy . . . one that was regarding it with dark, blankly hostile eyes.

Without further warning, the bull charged towards the bear, its horns pointing straight ahead, like the tips of twin lances, the sand flying up in heavy clouds behind it. The bull was almost upon its enemy when the bear likewise began to charge. The spectators howled yet louder, some already having made bets with each other as to which of the beasts would be victorious. At the last moment, the bear altered its course, swerving beyond reach of the bull's deadly horns. The bull, infuriated still further, skidded to a halt, snorting and panting. But the bear had already turned and now fell upon its adversary, its claws raking flesh, its powerful muzzle drawing hot blood from the bull's muscle-cloaked neck.

The sight of this scarlet cloud spraying into the humid air, the first bloodshed of the day, drew fevered screams and applause from the audience. The thirst for blood that had drawn them to the amphitheatre was made more intense by this first brief taste. Like the lover who catches a fleeting glimpse of his beloved's body, the flames of their passions were fanned deliciously, unbearably, and they screamed for more.

Further enraged by the pain of the bear's attack, the bull writhed madly, its muscles flexing like soft iron beneath its sweating skin. With the bear's weight upon it, the bull sank to the ground, but as the crowd leaned forward in anticipation of the kill, the magnificent beast found the strength it needed at the crucial moment. As the bear bit and bit again, its opponent clenched the muscles of its forelegs, arched its back and threw the bear from it. The spectators howled as the bull immediately turned and executed a short charge towards the bear, catching it in its mid-section and tossing it to one side in a single thrust. The bear landed badly in an explosion of sand and blood. A long gash had been opened in its side; the blood ran in rivulets through the forest of its dense fur. Stunned by the blow, it slowly raised itself to a standing position, the more to intimidate its snorting opponent. But the effort was too great, and it fell forward on all fours. Both badly wounded, the animals were now matched in weakness as they had before been in strength. They regarded each other for several moments, panting, snorting, their instinct for survival pulsing with the blood through their veins.

The next move was the bull's. It charged again, but this time it had not sufficient room to get up a good speed. The bear immediately launched itself at its enemy, falling between the deadly horns and clasping the bull around its neck with powerful forelegs. Once again it went to work on the already lacerated flesh as the bull, which, in rage and terror, dashed forward and backward, accelerating and sliding to a halt in a desperate effort to rid itself of its attacker.

The lustful eyes of the spectators followed this titanic struggle with glee; many panted almost in time with the beasts, although not in sympathy, but in expectation of the next gout of blood.

They were not to be disappointed. The furious motions of the bull's head finally dislodged the bear, and it slipped forward, its belly and chest sliding between the horns as it howled in fear and anger. Now its front paws clung desperately to the horns as it crouched upon the hot sand, literally face to face with its opponent. For a brief instant, the two animals' eyes met. For a brief instant, a primal contact was made, and something passed between them, something far beyond the comprehension of the humans watching avidly from all sides. Perhaps it was despair, perhaps an instinctive recognition that death stalked them both even as they stalked each other.

An instant of dreamlike stillness, and then the bear struck. With a lightning-fast movement, its head snapped forward and its powerful jaws closed around the bull's dripping snout. The bull howled in agony as the yellow teeth crushed flesh, bone and cartilage into a bloody, shapeless pulp. As the bull drew itself back, staggering, disoriented and crippled by the pain flooding its head, the crowd screamed, laughed and pointed to the crimson fountain issuing in an unstoppable flow from the ragged hole where its snout had been.

The bear, sensing that its adversary was close to death, gathered its strength for the final assault and lunged forward; but the bull knew also, and in a last desperate movement – the only one it had the strength left to make – it moved its head up and to one side, presenting a single horn to the onrushing bear. Carried forward by its momentum, the bear could not stop. It impaled itself on the horn, screamed in agony and fell sideways. The horn ripped open its belly, exposing its internal organs, which tumbled out as the defeated animal crashed to the sand. Now a barely recognisable lump of fur, blood and glistening red and purple entrails, the bear panted out its last breath, and lay still.

The bull had likewise fallen to its side in the red-stained sand, but still there was life left in it. The spectators cheered and applauded in appreciation of a grand battle, and then waited as two *confectores* carrying swords entered the arena. One approached the still bear, the other the panting bull. With well-practised thrusts, each man plunged his sword through the animal's head, splitting its brain and ending its life instantly. This titanic struggle had been merely a foretaste of what was to come, a trifle to whet the appetites of the spectators, who now sat panting as the two animals had panted in their rage and terror, grinning as only human beings can grin. The carcasses of the bull and bear were dragged away in preparation for the next stage of the *venatio*.

The crowd exploded in cheers and applause as fifty *venatores* entered the arena. These were the men who would be facing the wild animals in combat. Some wore close-fitting tunics and carried the *venabulum*, or iron-pointed hunting spear; others were similarly attired and carried bows and quivers of arrows; still other *venatores* wore iron plates over their chests, *galera* (fringed guards) upon their shoulders, and carried swords.

A group of slaves dragged a *cochlea* to the centre of the arena, and made certain that its wooden base was planted firmly upon the sand. This revolving device, twice the height of a man, would give any *venator* who chose to use it some protection by confusing a charging animal.

The gates in the *podium* slid up, and a multitude of animals entered the arena. All were destined to meet their ends here. There were elephants and rhinoceroses, lions, tigers and panthers, gazelles, deer and antelope, more bulls and more bears. Amongst this vast and variegated assortment of animals a score of hunting dogs ran; they would accompany the *venatores* on their mission of slaughter.

The scene that unfolded then, before the rapt eyes of the spectators, was the very embodiment of chaos. Carnage became a state of being, an order of reality unto itself, a universe of blood and mayhem contained within the pristine ellipse of the amphitheatre. In the streets outside, the philosophers and thieves went about their business through the empty streets of the city.

Occasionally one would glance in the direction of the gargantuan travertine edifice in the distance, momentarily distracted by the ululation of the mob within as it demonstrated its approval of a particularly toothsome atrocity.

Within the arena, a hunting dog brought down a gazelle and was quickly joined by its fellows, converging on the unfortunate animal – its brown eyes empty of all but terror – and tearing it asunder. A few paces away, a *venator* took aim with his bow and let fly an arrow directly between the eyes of a charging lion. Reduced instantly from a magnificent beast to a lifeless carcass, the lion ploughed a blood-stained furrow into the sand. A panther, all sleek and speeding muscle, leaped over the lion's prone body in its pursuit of another *venator* who had already loosed his spear at his quarry and missed. The panther flew at the running man, bringing him down with the consummate ease of this great hunting species. Its front legs outstretched, the panther opened its jaws wide, and with a single bite took away his face. This drew the attention of the spectators on this side of the arena, their eyes fixed immovably on the enraged panther as it bit again and again. Some turned to each other, asking excitedly whether the man was still alive and trying to fend off his attacker. Their companions laughed and replied that this was impossible: his head was virtually gone. His movements, they stated with the pomposity of those who had seen this sort of thing many times before, were merely the spasmodic thrashings of a half-destroyed corpse.

Elsewhere, in a variation of the first encounter of the day, a bull and bear were chained together to increase their fury. The savagery of their battle was thus increased tenfold as neither was able to retreat, nor avoid the onslaught of the other. The spectators closest to these animals screamed in excited appreciation as the bear tore chunks of living flesh from its opponent, before receiving an up-thrust horn through its lower jaw that caused it to drop dead to the floor.

Near the centre of the arena another bear, driven to distraction by a hunting dog, seized the animal around the neck and shook it so violently that in a few seconds the jaws met each other and the dog's head flew spinning into the air. Not content with having killed its tormentor, the bear went to work with tooth and claw upon the dog's torso, opening it with a single stroke and snapping at the gouts of blood that sprayed into the air.

When the body had been reduced to bones and jelly, the bear looked up at the *cochlea* that had been set wildly spinning by a *venator* trying to avoid the claws of an attacking tiger. Momentarily startled by this strange contrivance, the bear retreated until it caught sight of something that spurred it to new heights of insensate rage: a rhinoceros, a normally peaceful creature that had itself been tormented into a fury by a group of trembling *magistri*, who had been goading it with whips and flaming straw. With a sideways flick of its great horned head, it caught one of the *magistri* and sent him hurtling into the marble of the *podium*, the impact smashing his skull open and eliciting hoots of derisive laughter from the nearby spectators.

The rhinoceros turned away from the remaining *magistri* as the bear began a howling charge towards it. Some of the spectators threw up their hands in exasperation at this, for they knew well from many previous *venationes* that a bear was no match for the rhinoceros, a great, horned engine of destruction. This particular battle, they knew, was decided before it had even begun, so they shrugged their shoulders and watched the inevitable outcome. The rhinoceros charged towards the onrushing bear. Adamantine armour met soft flesh, and the bear was tossed like a straw dummy high into the air. Landing with bone-snapping force upon the sand, the hapless beast could do nothing to avoid the second charge of the rhinoceros, whose horn struck it square in the belly. It was only with half-hearted cheers that the spectators greeted the eruption of blood and intestines, the smears of carrion that now coated the head of the rhinoceros.

A DAY AT THE GAMES

The cheers grew suddenly in enthusiasm, however, when the crowd realised that the rhinoceros was not slowing down, but continuing with its charge, directly towards a helmeted *venator* who had his back turned to it, his attention being fixed on an elephant, whose side he was attempting to pierce with his sword. In the brief seconds that followed as the rhinoceros closed in upon the *venator*, who was still oblivious to the destruction pounding towards him, the spectators drew in their breath, savouring the approaching moment as they might a delicious wine.

The elephant drew back from the *venator* as it saw the path the rhinoceros was taking. At the same time, the *venator* became aware of a deep, ominous sound pulsing through the metal of his helmet. He was experienced enough to realise that this was the sound of hooves on sand; experienced enough to realise that no gazelle was making that sound; experienced enough to know that he was already dead.

He had not even time to turn as the great horned head of the rhinoceros ploughed squarely into his back, shattering his spine and blowing the pearl-white fragments out through his exploding chest. Now exhausted, the gore-covered rhinoceros drew to a halt, while the spectators screamed in vain at the remaining *venatores* to destroy the animal.

The survivors had their hands full, however. Another armoured *venator* was on his knees near the Emperor's box, only his shield standing between him and the crushing weight of a lion. Commodus watched, his face contorted in a rictus of bloodthirsty mirth as the lion ripped pieces of wood and leather from the *venator*'s shield. Now bent almost completely backward, the fighter swung his sword arm with increasing desperation, looking for a vulnerable spot on the big cat's belly. Long, yellow, blood-stained teeth now began to snap like the crack of a whip, closer and closer to the helmeted head. Commodus leaned forward on his seat, craning his neck to get a better view of the lion's jaws as they finally found purchase on the *venator*'s helmet and ripped it from his head, revealing a face set in stern resolution. The Emperor turned to a companion, and commented favourably on the man's lack of fear. The *venatores*, like their gladiator counterparts who would be doing battle in the afternoon, were taught to cultivate a total contempt for fear and death, however violent.

Finally, as the lion's great, maned head drew close for the kill, its hot breath enveloping the *venator*'s sweating brow, his sword at last found its mark and plunged deep into the animal's ribcage. As the lion arched its back, spitting and roaring in agony, the *venator* abandoned his shield, rolled out from under the contorting beast and buried his sword again and again in its neck.

When the lion's last breath had rattled from its blood-filled maw, the *venator* stood and looked triumphantly up at his Emperor. This was a most unwise decision, for Commodus had been looking forward to watching the lion take the *venator*'s head from his shoulders; now, as he caught sight of the man's smiling face looking up at him, Commodus' disappointment turned to furious indignation. Almost immediately, the *venator* realised his mistake, but it was far, far too late. Reaching down, Commodus picked up a bow and an arrow from the full quiver beside his seat. In one swift, clean movement, he took aim and fired an arrow through the *venator*'s neck, killing him instantly. Casting the bow aside in disgust, Commodus reclined in his seat and tried to concentrate on the rest of the *venatio*, but he was now out of sorts, and began to dwell on the *venator*'s insolence. His mood grew darker as midday approached. He hoped the lunchtime executions would lighten his spirits, but he doubted it. He resigned himself to the fact that he would have to enter the arena himself this afternoon, to take on some of the gladiators and, in ending their lives, palliate his temper.

Meanwhile, the *venatio* was proceeding splendidly. The arena was awash with blood, the running feet of the *venatores* kicking up huge gobbets of wet sand as they raced towards their next victim. Their bodies glistened with a pink sheen of blood and sweat, their muscles rippling cords, straining ever harder to continue the slaughter, fatigue now as deadly an enemy as any wild cat or rampaging bull. Their headlong dashes across the red-streaked sand were followed most ardently by the dignitaries' wives, whose transportations of lust where just beginning, and would not reach their crescendo until late in the afternoon, when the gladiators had displayed their prowess before their wide and lascivious eyes.

Here and there lay the huge, unmoving bodies of elephants and rhinoceroses, like islands in some strange, ochre lake. The gazelles and antelopes had long since been despatched, their opened carcasses picked at occasionally by the surviving dogs. Lions and panthers, lords of their own realms, lay as charnel wreckage across the arena floor, their pelts split by sword and lance and arrow.

But the *venatio* was not done yet. The spectators clamoured for more, and more they would have. The doors in the *podium* opened again and again, disgorging more ferocious cats, more bulls and bears, more elephants, more defenceless gazelles. At one stage, a group of five lions entered the arena and imme-diately lay down, refusing to fight. This brought screams of derisive laughter from the spectators. Other lions could be seen inside the openings in the *podium*: they refused even to come out into the open. This caused some confusion among the *venatores*, who killed the prone lions almost with embarrass-ment to the jeering of the crowd. Those lions that cowered within the *podium* openings were killed with arrows from a distance.

Meanwhile, in the mêlée proper, a *venator* found himself the object of a tiger's attention. It pounced forward with glorious, terrifying speed. The *venator*, who had already fired his last arrow, was in a bad position. Glancing desperately behind him, he saw that the *cochlea* was just a few paces away, left spinning by the last man to use it, who was now nowhere to be seen.

He fancied he could feel the tiger's breath on the back of his neck as he dashed across the sand to the only refuge in the entire arena. As he reached the *cochlea*, the *venator* tripped and fell headlong to the floor, taking in a mouthful of blood-soaked sand. Retching at the thought of what the sand contained, he scrambled behind the *cochlea*. Coughing and spitting, he desperately span the device faster.

The tiger skidded to a halt, tale wagging furiously to and fro, jaws dripping saliva. Its quarry had disappeared, and now all it could see was this . . . thing, this spinning thing. Was it dangerous? Could it be eaten? Pacing back and forward in front of the *cochlea*, the powerful predator regarded the contraption uneasily, its attention frequently distracted by the slaughter going on around it.

Another *venator*, his confidence brimming after many kills, ran screaming at the beast, both hands gripping the shaft of his *venabulum*. But the big cat, alerted by his foolish cries, span around instantly, its jaws wide. With a single swipe of its huge paw it split the *venabulum* as if it were a twig, and lunged. Still carried forward by his momentum, the *venator* ran straight into the tiger's jaws, which closed about his head and reduced him in an instant to a lifeless rag doll.

Peering from behind the spinning *cochlea*, the other *venator* watched his fellow's death, his eyes wide, his heartbeat like thunder in his chest. The tiger, done with one of its enemies, now returned its attention to the whirling contraption. It sensed that a prey animal was still cowering behind it, and so began a slow stalk in a wide arc around the machine. Behind him, the *venator* could hear the shouts from the first few ranks of spectators thirteen feet above. They suspected that he had lost his nerve, that fear had overcome him. The spectators were seldom wrong, for they knew well the stench of fear from the thousands of criminals who were routinely executed here. His hesitant movements, the way his hand shook as he wiped the stinging sweat from his face, the wide-eyed and desperate expression that contorted his features; all combined to betray his inner feelings to the spectators. Outraged that this man had succumbed to terror, they began to shout abuse at him, screaming at him that he was a coward, a pathetic child no better than the hunting dogs that fought each other over the scraps of gazelle meat.

Although seized with fear as he watched the snarling head of the great striped demon appear from behind the *cochlea*, the *venator* yet felt shame at the spectators' taunts. His eyes met the tiger's as the huge cat paused. The shouts from behind and above him seemed to fade as he gazed at this graceful feline destroyer. Indeed, all sounds of the arena were swallowed and stifled by the sound of his own heartbeat, the rush of fevered blood a hissing cataract within his head. The moment stretched like a straining tendon. Man and tiger regarded each other as if they were the last representatives of two armies that had been engaged in a titanic struggle since the beginning of time. The *venator* gazed into his adversary's eyes, suddenly and inappropriately struck by their terrible beauty. Eyes like portals revealing the hunter's powerful soul. Eternal eyes, revealing the eternity of death. Precious stones decorating the sepulchre.

There had been many last moments, for man and animal alike, on this fine morning. Death hung over the arena like an invisible cloud. The *venator* lowered his eyes from those of the tiger, as the screams of the spectators again impinged upon his consciousness. Was this to be his last moment?

As his gaze dropped to the floor, something caught his attention: a glint in his peripheral vision. Snapping his head to the left, he saw it – the blade of a sword half buried in the sand just a few paces away. Its owner was gone, perhaps to the far side of the arena, perhaps much, much further. His own instinct for survival, as strong as the tiger's, took over and forced his tired muscles to flex one more time, to take this last chance against death.

With a desperate effort, he lunged to his left. In the same instant, the tiger lunged also, launching itself like a living spear towards him. The *venator* thrust his hand deep into the sand, found the hilt of the abandoned sword and brought the weapon up, twisting onto his back as he did so. The crowd shouted their approval, gratified that the *venator* had found his courage and would not, after all, meet his death in disgrace.

The great beast flew through the air, descending on its prey, bringing all its power to bear in this final, death-dealing manoeuvre. Had it seen the up-thrust sword, it would still not have been able to alter its course. The tiger fell upon man and sword, the blade finding its mark even as the tiger's paw covered the *venator*'s head, snapping it back and breaking his neck. The *venator* died instantly, one of the least painful deaths of the entire morning. His sword buried itself in the tiger's heart. With a final scream, the big cat collapsed upon the body of the *venator*. The final moment had belonged to each of them.

As midday approached, the *venatio* drew to a close. It had been a bad day for the *venatores*: a greater than average number had met their ends on this occasion. Those who remained finished off the few surviving animals – a pair of wounded lions, an elephant covered with lacerations that held up its trunk in lamentation as a spear pierced its eye.

As the *venatores* finally left the arena to the cheers and applause of the spectators, large numbers of slaves entered to haul away the carcasses – both animal and human – and turn over the blood soaked top layer of sand. By the time they had finished, the arena looked as if nothing had happened. The hot and thirsty spectators were then sprayed with perfumed water from the intricate system of pipes that extended like blood vessels beneath the *cavea*, as they sat back and discussed with each other the spectacle they had just enjoyed. In spite of the carnage to which they had been witness, the crowd had not had their fill. There was far more death to savour, more blood to come, and they awaited it in good humour.

THE LUNCHTIME EXECUTIONS

In truth, the spectators had not seen the last of the wild animals for that day: a few beasts would be called upon to perform another service in the arena, that of executioners. Preparations were made for those slaves and criminals who had been condemned to execution *ad bestias*. This, however, was not the only manner of execution to be practised. The cruelty of the arena would take many forms.

At this point, many spectators left the arena to take some lunch; but many remained, most of whom were plebeians occupying free seats. They had queued since midnight the previous night for these, camping out beneath the stars, trying not to make too much noise, lest they disturb the Emperor's horses and be beaten away. Now they retained their seats, since giving them up for a meagre lunch would almost certainly mean losing them when the arena filled up for the afternoon spectacles. Thus the amphitheatre remained occupied by many, who required entertainment in the interlude between the *venatio* and the afternoon's *munus*.

The ragged and bloodthirsty crowd knew that the condemned were already in the amphitheatre: the heavy carts had brought them here earlier, moving slowly through the streets of Rome in a long convoy of misery, accompanied by marching guards. These men had not the presence of mind – or indeed the courage – of the slave Attalus, who had already departed this world in an awful but swift manner, and who was now safe at last. The carts at the head of the convoy had held freeborn men condemned to death for crimes such as murder, arson and armed robbery. The carts behind held those of a lower rank: slaves, deserters and freed men. Having been sentenced in their various provinces, they had come to Rome from all over the Empire, to meet their ends in the most appalling fashion, to the cheers and laughter of the spectators, their final moments no more than a brief interlude on a day of savagery.

First, though, there would be a few minutes of farce, performed by the *paegniarii*, idiotic players whose bodies were covered with crude bandages, and who fought each other with staffs, whips and shields. Their combats were a joke, and were intended as such. Staggering about the arena, they beat and flogged each other (none of these injuries were life-threatening, or even particularly serious) in knockabout entertainment.

This comedic display did not last long, for it was violent death that the spectators were here to see. The *paegniarii* left the arena to half-hearted applause, and the first of the condemned entered. Although there were only two men here, there were many others waiting in the warren of corridors and cells beneath the arena floor. These were *noxii ad gladium ludi damnati*, condemned to die by the blade, free men who had become criminals, and were therefore allowed to die by means of a noble weapon.

The first two stood facing each other in the arena. Neither of them had any gladiatorial training, neither wore any armour, and only one held a dagger. It was thus virtually certain that the armed man would kill his opponent. Both men understood this, and so the unarmed man decided, with the swiftness of the survival instinct, that the only thing to do was to run from his opponent as fast as he could. This he did, taking off across the sand and eliciting shouts of disapproval from the spectators.

Almost at once, a large group of servants appeared, carrying whips and glowing branding irons. They closed in upon the fleeing man and went to work on him, the sound of cracking whips and the smoke rising from burning flesh placating the crowd. The unarmed man, clutching a badly scorched arm and with ugly red welts across his back, was driven towards his waiting opponent. The battle was short-lived: the dagger-wielder lunged and planted his weapon in the centre of the other's chest, cleaving his breast bone. He dropped without a sound, and was hauled away by means of a long staff with a sharp hook at the end, which further outraged his tortured flesh.

Another condemned criminal then entered the arena; the first was forced to surrender his weapon to him, and become the defenceless quarry. It was not long before he, too, lay on the sand, his neck open and pumping out blood. The process was repeated: the victor surrendered the dagger to the newest arrival. This time, the dagger-wielder hesitated to attack. Perhaps he knew his unarmed foe; perhaps he dreaded the thought of taking a life almost as much as he dreaded the thought of losing his own; perhaps he delayed in a desperate attempt to prolong his life for just a few more fleeting moments, knowing full well that victory would herald nothing but his own demise.

At any rate, he refused to strike the fatal blow. In spite of the fact that they had witnessed this despairing tactic on many previous occasions (or perhaps because of it), the crowd roared once again, spitting vitriol at the hapless dagger-wielder. The servants approached, drawing pictograms of cruelty across his back with their whips, goading him on with the agonising touch of their branding irons. Tears flowed down his cheeks, fear, pain and misery their ingredients, as he followed the only course of action open to him and began to slash wildly at his opponent. There was none of the skill, none of the finesse of true gladiatorial combat here, only the wildly arcing knife, only the necessity to kill as quickly as possible before being killed.

With ease, the knife opened the unarmed man's belly, and the crowd applauded as his entrails spilled out and mingled with the sand. Falling to his knees, the dying man looked up at his killer, whose own face was contorted at the enormity of what he had done, and of what would soon be done to him. The dying man tried to smile, for peace would soon be upon him, terror and pain at last at an end. He failed, and fell forward into the warm pool of his blood.

This slaughter continued for some time, following the same pattern, until only one criminal was left. Since there were no foes remaining to be handed the knife, a *confector* (who was also charged with the killing of wounded animals during the *venatio*) therefore moved up behind him and cut his throat. Thus ended the first phase of the programme of executions.

Next came those convicted of a variety of crimes, but whose status in society precluded their dying by the blade. One by one, the condemned were led out into the arena. The first was a slave who had drawn a knife across his master's throat one night. He appeared, tied with his hands behind his back to a wooden stake affixed to a small chariot, which two servants wheeled to the centre of the arena. The slave, naked except for a loin-cloth, looked around him with wide, terror-filled eyes, his ears assaulted by the screams of indignation issuing from the spectators. His gaze flitted from opening to opening in the *podium*. Seeing this, some of the spectators joked to each other that he was wondering from which direction his death would come.

The question was soon answered. To the slave's right, a door slid up and a single lion moved tentatively into the arena, glancing around at the roaring crowd in much the same way as the slave had done. The attendants had already retreated to a safe distance, leaving the condemned man alone with his inevitable destroyer. The animal continued in its slow, almost hesitant gait. For a moment, the attendants, dressed only in tunics, wondered apprehensively whether they would be required to force it with whips to attack.

But the lion continued to move towards the trembling man. What he experienced, coming face to face with death incarnated in an invincible beast, can scarcely be imagined. Perhaps thought itself ceased, driven from his mind by his own animal terror. Perhaps one of the philosophers strolling through the streets of Rome might have been able to guess at his state of mind as he was about to be ripped asunder in an explosion of blood and agony. But for the spectators watching these events, this was of no significance whatsoever. There was only one fact worth considering: this man and the others who would follow were meeting justice for the crimes they had committed. It was fitting punishment, and no more.

When it had come to within about thirty paces of the little chariot, the beast roared once and broke into the short run that would bring it to its quarry. It leaped upon the man, the weight of its muscular bulk instantly snapping both the stake affixed to the chariot, and the man's pelvis. Unfortunately for him, this was not nearly enough to kill him. The two fell upon the chariot, splitting it into a hundred fragments that pierced the man's back and sent additional lances of agony through his torso. The lion bit deep and snapped its head from side to side, its magnificent mane like a great, ochre cloud around its snarling head. His body opened, the quivering meat was exposed and the man lay like a flower that had bloomed in an instant, all red jelly and pale sinew.

While the lion was driven back towards the *podium* with whips and burning straw, the leftovers from its meal were dragged from the arena, as the crowd settled down to prepare itself for the next display.

The eyes of the spectators were instantly drawn to one of the large trapdoors in the arena floor, which now slid slowly aside, revealing a dark, ominous space, a veritable pit of despair. A low, rumbling murmur spread among them, mingling with the sinister clatter of the heavy chains pulling the platform and raising it into view. Upon this platform stood a large wooden frame, composed of two uprights and a cross-beam. From the cross-beam a man hung upside-down, naked but for a soiled loincloth. The coarse ropes binding his feet had already begun to cut into his ankles, causing rivulets of blood to run up his legs, the ugly wounds only made worse by his desperate struggling. His hands were bound tightly behind his back, and the taught muscles in his arms glistened with sweat and dirt in the hard sunlight. Escape was utterly impossible, and yet he continued to struggle, his instinct for survival overwhelming every other thought in his mind. He knew well enough what was about to happen. He was about to make atonement for his life as a brigand in the countryside around Rome. In his time, he had caused much pain and suffering to those he had waylaid. Now, that pain, that suffering, was about to be repaid to him a thousandfold.

Blinking furiously against the stinging sweat that dripped into his eyes, the brigand snapped his head around frantically. From his inverted position the amphitheatre, with its tier upon tier of rapt faces, the rumble issuing from their lips growing ever greater in intensity, seemed like the very ceiling of the underworld; the wide circle of sky at the centre of the vast awning like the mouth of Death itself. As his eyes flitted between the gates in the *podium*, the brigand prayed that Nature, too, might be inverted, that the ropes binding him might break, and that he might fall away from the arena, into the bright blue circle, into eternal freedom . . .

The crowd began to roar, and the brigand knew that his final moments were upon him. He knew also that they promised to be the longest moments of his life. He fought against the instinct to shut his eyes tight, and continued to snap his head around, trying to see from which direction the horror would come.

It came from three directions at once: three of the gates had been raised, allowing three panthers to enter the arena, their elegant black forms like nightmares in flesh and fur. They saw their prey instantly and, having been starved for many days, instantly converged upon it. The jaws of the first panther closed around the brigand's left arm, pulling it from its socket with all the ease of a gourmand ripping a leg from a roasted chicken. The beast then tried to make off with its prize, only to be frustrated by the fact that its meal was still tied to the right arm by the rope bindings. Infuriated, the big cat thrashed its sleek head from side to side and pulled with all its might, the muscles in its front legs rippling. The brigand was spun around at the hips, his right arm dislocated at the shoulder, the discs in his spine popping out, the vertebrae grinding against each other. His screams rose into the humid air of the amphitheatre, mingling with the roar of the crowd, one voice against thousands.

The panther finally won its battle with the man's flesh: his right arm came away, leaving his torso to pump blood from its two gaping wounds with their quivering ribbons of crimson meat. For the briefest of moments, the other two panthers considered challenging their fellow for his meal; but in truth there was little point, and so they busied themselves with the task of despatching the writhing animal hanging from the cross-beam.

The brigand's final scream was so powerful that it shredded his vocal chords; the last sound he made was a feeble, high whistle which momentarily perplexed his destroyers, before one opened his belly with its claws, and the other took away his face. What remained was pulled from the beams and devoured in short order.

The crowd applauded loudly as the panthers were finally driven back to the openings in the *podium*, while the wooden frame sank once more into the blood-spattered arena floor.

The next display was a firm favourite with the crowd, since it demonstrated a certain amount of dexterity on the part of the condemned, with the added *frisson* that this dexterity could only result in a terrible death.

Driven by whip and branding iron, the next man lurched into the arena. Like his predecessors, he was dressed only in a loincloth; but this man carried with him a long, thin staff, which ended in a hook. He stood in the centre of the arena and looked around at the dark openings in the *podium*. Like the previous man, he was a brigand; like the previous man, he glanced frantically from opening to opening, trying to see which of them would disgorge his death. Unlike the previous man, he had no trouble in finding the direction on which to concentrate his attention. Within the arch beneath the Emperor's platform he could clearly discern two huge, dark bulks already committing frightful violence upon one another, roaring and snorting in a confusion of limbs and torsos. The gate slid up with a rattle, and into the arena spilled two dreadful incarnations of raw power.

The bull and the bear had been bound to each other with a ten-foot metal chain. Infuriated, they fell upon each other again and again, their attempts to escape constantly frustrated, the adamantine links refusing to break and liberate them. It was the task of the condemned man to thrust his staff at the collar of either beast, and to unhook the chain that bound them together.

In abject terror, he approached the pair, to shouted abuse and taunts from the crowd, their shouts to get on with it pounding in his ears. Of course, the hideously animated tangle of gigantic, muscle-cloaked bodies made this impossible, unless he wished to end his life immediately. The survival instinct, however, could be counted on to prolong the affair, as the trembling, sweating man approached and retreated again and again. The bull and bear, their attentions very firmly fixed upon one another, ignored him, and continued their titanic struggle.

This could not continue for very long, and so the crowd contented themselves with watching the battle of the two great beasts, occasionally hurling an insult at the hapless criminal, and waiting for the animals to begin tiring. When this happened, they knew, the condemned would be afforded an opportunity of approaching the monsters more closely . . . close enough to use the hooked staff.

It did not take long for the beasts' constantly straining

muscles to tire. Presently, the ferocity of their combat grew less, as they parted as far as the sturdy chain would allow, and regarded each other with breathless fury and hatred. The condemned took his chance, and made a darting approach towards the bear, which he judged to be a little weaker than its enemy. Reaching out with the staff, he aimed its hooked end at the iron ring upon its wide collar. The bear saw him, however, and swiped at him with a powerful fore-leg. Ducking just in time, the criminal scampered away to safety, much to the annoyance of the spectators, who loudly berated him for his cowardice from the security of the *cavea*.

The bear's action had goaded the bull into further fury, and it charged its opponent with all the force it could muster. Once again, the beasts went at each other, their gyrating bodies and flailing limbs producing an ungainly dance of blood, fur and flying slobber. From one side of the arena to the other they went, kicking up great, heavy clouds of sand and dust, while the tiny, frail figure of the condemned continued to dodge their flying bulks. Again and again he tried to unhook the chain that bound them to each other, in the awful knowledge his only other alternative was death by whip and branding iron.

Tears of fear and frustration coursing down his cheeks, filthy with his own sweat and the blood and saliva of the beasts, the criminal fell to the sand in exhaustion as the spectators threw up their hands in exasperation at his pitiful lack of mettle. The attendants lost no time in entering the arena once again, and with whip and branding iron, offered him powerful persuasion to continue with his task.

His back covered with welts, his left arm blackened and smoking from the attentions of the branding iron, he dragged himself to his feet, and with one enormous final effort lunged at the bull's collar. The crowd would have called it a lucky move; the condemned would doubtless have described it otherwise. As he ploughed headlong into the sand, the hook on the end of his staff found its target, and the chain fell away from the angry, snorting bull.

An ear-shattering cheer went up from the spectators, as the criminal, in utter despair, watched the enormous beasts dash apart from each other. He knew well what would happen next. The arena attendants ran for their lives as the bull and bear now focused their attentions on the puny creature that had been flitting here and there during their battle. Both had sustained serious wounds during their confinement by the chain, but not nearly serious enough to prevent them from destroying the exhausted human being still lying between them.

While the bear sat down upon the hot sand to gather its breath, the bull charged and tossed the criminal into the air. His ribcage shattered on contact, the condemned man fell back to the floor and lay still. It was all he could do to continue breathing as the blood from his punctured lungs filled his mouth and exited his body in a fine, delicate red mist.

As the bull withdrew, preparing to charge again, the bear, now recovered somewhat, took its opportunity and ran headlong at the prone form. In a whirlwind of teeth and claws it descended upon the defenceless man and tore him asunder. What remained of him was tossed into the air and trampled into the sand as the beasts again took up their battle. By the time they had wounded and exhausted each other sufficiently for the *confectores* to approach and put them both to death, nothing remained of the criminal but pieces of skin, bone and a few crimson gobbets of carrion.

The next execution spectacle came immediately, to the delight of the crowd whose bloodlust was well and truly manifest. To screams and shouts and riotous applause, another bull entered the arena. Strapped to its back was a woman, an adulteress, naked but for a loincloth, her hands bound behind her back.

Her screams of terror drew contemptuous laughter from the

cavea as she was thrown to and fro upon the great, arching back of the brute. At one point, thrown violently forward as the bull tried to rid itself of the annoyance on its back, the woman's face smashed against its powerful neck, destroying her nose in a sudden spray of blood. Her head lolled back upon her shoulders as she spat a miniature fountain of blood and shattered teeth into the air.

Growing more and more infuriated, the bull dashed from one side of the arena to the other, jumping high into the air and kicking wildly, the hapless woman's blood-spattered form growing indistinct, so violently was it thrown from side to side, forwards and backwards. Her screams had ceased as the air was repeatedly knocked from her straining lungs, and it was all she could do to keep breathing.

The crowd groaned with a terrible pleasure as the blood flowed copiously from the woman's ruined face over her heaving chest, and mingled with the sweat on the rippling muscles of the bull's back. This dance of agony continued for several more minutes, until one of the leather straps holding the woman in place finally snapped, and she fell to one side. But there was to be no escape, for the remaining straps held, and so she was trapped beneath the great belly of the beast as it continued to run and jump and kick.

Her sweating, blooded limbs flailing wildly, her head ploughing repeatedly into the sand, the condemned was battered and buffeted from hind legs to forelegs, as the bull grew yet more enraged with its unseen burden. Finally, it came to a halt and drew back a little. Now it could see the woman, lying half dead on the sand in front of it, her body caked with blood and covered with purple bruises, her arms and legs now dislocated and lying at grotesque angles. Snorting and moaning, the beast inclined its head and thrust its horns downward again and again, as the spectators leaned forward, cheered and applauded.

The arena was cleared once again in preparation for the final executions this lunchtime. The four great trapdoors in the arena floor slowly drew aside to allow the platforms beneath to be raised into the open. When they saw what the platforms held, the crowd broke into enthusiastic applause once again.

Upon each platform had been erected a wooden cross, from which hung a condemned man. All four were arsonists, whose crimes had been committed at Brundisium and Capua in the south, Aquileia in the north, and at Rome. They each wore a tunic, but it was no ordinary tunic: it was black, and glistened in the sunlight. Each of the condemned wore the *tunica molesta*: the garments had been soaked in pitch. The arsonists were to be punished according to the nature of their crimes; they were condemned *ad flammas* . . . they were to be burned alive in the arena.

When they saw the four *confectores* entering the arena, the condemned started to scream and moan, begging the crowd for mercy. The crowd screamed back at them. They turned to the Emperor, their faces contorted in terror. Commodus merely smiled, gave them a friendly wave, and sat back comfortably.

Each *confector* carried a burning torch, which would be touched to the *tunica molesta* of each criminal. As they watched the approach of the *confectores*, two of the condemned lost control of their bowels. When he saw the faeces running down their legs, Commodus turned to those nearest him with an indulgent smile, as if sharing in some witticism at a theatrical performance.

The time of their death was now upon them. The torches of the *confectores* touched their pitch-soaked clothes, and the flames sprang to them, as if escaping imprisonment. Wrapped in cloaks of fire, the condemned began to scream as the burning pitch closed upon their flesh. Four columns of black smoke rose into the air above the arena. In revolting agony the bodies of the condemned writhed; in excitement and hilarity writhed those of the spectators. Skulls split with the heat, revealing the grey pulp within; stomachs burst, disgorging boiling entrails. The awful stench of roasting flesh filled the arena. Presently, the screams ceased, and the only sound that could be heard, other than the shouts of the crowd, was the crackle of the ravenous flames.

THE AFTERNOON BATTLES

In spite of the great popularity of the *venatio* and the executions, the gladiatorial battles of the afternoon were still the high point of the day for most spectators. Their excitement and enthusiasm were unabated as they discussed noisily the coming *munus*, while groups of slaves once again cleared away the debris from the arena.

When this job had been done, the p*ompa* began. In this grand procession, all the gladiators who would be fighting this afternoon entered through the great arch on the arena's long axis, wearing sumptuous, brightly coloured costumes. This procession was all that remained of the original purpose of gladiatorial combats, a duty paid to the illustrious dead. The crowd continued to shout and applaud as they searched the group, trying to pick out their particular favourites. The gladiators made their circuit of the arena, passing the Emperor's box, from which Commodus watched them with unblinking eyes.

When the circuit had been completed, there followed two extremely important activities. The first was the drawing of lots. Although the *libellus numerarius*, which most of the spectators held in their hands, listed the names of the gladiators who were to fight this afternoon, it did not say who was to fight whom, or in what order. In fact, the only other information it contained was a symbol next to each gladiator's name, allowing the reader to see at a glance how well he had performed in the past. V stood for *victor*, meaning the defeat of an opponent; and M stood for *missus*, meaning he had lost but had fought well enough to be allowed to live. Elsewhere, on inscriptions marking the achievements of various gladiators, these symbols were repeated, and also included the Greek letter *theta* (Θ) to denote a gladiator who had lost his life.

The lots were drawn under the watchful eye of Commodus to establish which gladiators would be fighting each other. Account was, of course, taken of the varying skill levels of the gladiators: it would not have made for a very interesting spectacle were a novice to have been pitted against a veteran with ten or twenty victories to his name. It would indeed have been a dishonour upon the more experienced man (in Pompeii, many years before, a wit had drawn upon a wall an ironic illustration of this important rule. The drawing was of two gladiators, one of whom, a *retiarius* named Antigonus, claimed a ludicrous 2,112 victories while his opponent, Superbus, claimed only one).

When the lots had been drawn and the gladiators now knew who would be facing whom in the arena, the second important activity began: the *probatio armorum*, or inspection of arms. This was made by Commodus himself, who carefully checked every sword, every trident, every arrow for sharpness and straightness. Far from being bored by this meticulous inspection, most members of the crowd watched it with great attentiveness, for it ensured that all the gladiators would be fighting with the very best of weapons, and thus that each contest would be decided by the skill of the fighters rather than the quality of their tools.

As the *probatio armorum* continued, the gladiators busied themselves here and there in the arena with various warming-up exercises. This had the three-fold effect of loosening their muscles in preparation for deadly activity, occupying the several nerve-wracking minutes before the first contest, and giving the crowd something else to watch. The gladiators threw shields high into the air and caught them again, and launched spears and javelins with the greatest of elegance. Others practised their fighting manoeuvres with blunted weapons. Occasionally, an amateur would enter the arena to join the gladiators briefly in their practice. This drew appreciative applause from the more charitable spectators, and hoots of derision from others.

Presently, when the Emperor had finished his inspection, satisfied with the murderous quality of the weapons, the blunted practice arms were exchanged for the real ones, the amateurs hurried away and the trumpets sounded for the first combat to begin.

The first two gladiators of the afternoon walked to the centre of the vast, sand-filled arena. As they walked, the crowd exploded once again in jubilant applause, their cries now louder and more sustained than any that had risen from the *cavea* hitherto. The arrival of the musicians who would accompany the battles went almost unnoticed by the crowd. They carried their instruments, which included the *tuba*, the *organum* and the *lituus* to their assigned positions near the *podium* and prepared to perform their part in the great dramas that were to come.

The first man was a *retiarius*. Along with the net, with which he would attempt to trap and disable his opponent, he carried a trident. He was dressed only in a loose-fitting tunic: he possessed no armour whatsoever. While this clearly would allow him the advantage of great speed, he would need to avoid close quarters combat, keeping the trident at all times between himself and his adversary. Indeed, such was the retiarius' vulnerability that he occasionally fought from a raised dais, reached by a steep plank. While this afforded him a certain height advantage, however, it robbed him of his mobility. The dais would not be used today.

His opponent was the traditional one for a *retiarius*: a *secutor*, a type of gladiator known as a Samnite before the time of Augustus. The *secutor*, or 'pursuer', carried a rectangular shield and wore a visored helmet. He wore greaves to protect his lower legs, and a *manica* covered his sword arm. He was muscular and big-boned, easily strong enough to carry his heavy shield and slash with his sword for hours if necessary. His training in the *ludus* had included fighting with weapons heavier than the one he now carried, increasing his stamina considerably.

To anyone unfamiliar with the conventions of gladiatorial combat, it would have looked like a rather uneven match: the elegant, lightly-clad *retiarius* against the hulking, enormously strong *secutor*. But the spectators knew better, for they had seen this type of battle many times. As the opponents squared up to face each other, thousands of bets were made all over the *cavea*, and by no means all were laid in favour of the *secutor*.

The fight began with the *retiarius* immediately swinging his net around in a circular movement, and letting it fly at the *secutor*. The armoured gladiator foresaw this move, and brought his shield up even as the net left his opponent's hand. He held the shield at head level, at a shallow angle, and crouched, presenting a smaller target. Like some delicate but deadly creature from the depths of the ocean, the net glided over the shield of the *secutor* and on across the arena for many paces before soundlessly coming to rest upon the sand.

The music from the orchestra increased in tempo as the *retiarius* dashed across the arena away from the *secutor*. Once again, a visitor from a distant land, who had never seen a gladiatorial combat before, might have expected the crowd to boo and jeer at this act of apparent cowardice. But this was not the case. They understood that the *retiarius* was merely using one of his very few defensive weapons: his speed. They nodded and clapped as they watched the man hurtle across the hot sand, clearly planning how best to regain his net before the *secutor* intercepted and overpowered him.

As he reached a safe distance, the *retiarius* saw that he was in an awkward position: the *secutor* had not even bothered trying to give chase, but instead had merely walked across to the net. His tactic was obvious: he would wait by the net until the retiarius decided to come for it, which would not be too long, since the crowd quickly tired of stalemate situations. Sooner rather than later, the *retiarius* would have to make his move, and the secutor was absolutely ready for him.

Gripping the shaft of his trident firmly with both hands, the *retiarius* approached his enemy with a look of adamantine determination upon his already-sweating face. Of course, whatever expression the *secutor*'s face held was hidden by the perfectly smooth helmet he wore, although the *retiarius* did not doubt that it was as implacable as his own.

With a lightning-fast movement, the *retiarius* lunged with his trident, trying to force a way past his opponent's shield. From behind the shield the sword cut through the air in a tight, vicious arc. With a fraction of a second to spare, the *retiarius* whipped his trident to his right, swivelling his torso as he did so in an attempt to move his upper body out of the sword's path. This he did, but he had made a crucial mistake in not moving his whole body to the right, for the *secutor*'s sword continued in its arc and sliced neatly into the net-man's left thigh.

So sharp was the blade that he felt it only as a light caress. However, experience had taught him to glance down at his body whenever he felt a blow, in order instantly to assess the injury. When he did so this time, his heart sank: although the sword had not bitten deep enough to cripple him, it had taken away a sliver of flesh, revealing the bloody, purple mass of muscle beneath. His left leg would still carry him, but it would not be long before the blood loss caused lethal fatigue. As he jumped backwards out of reach of the next sword thrust, he realised that he would have to work fast.

For his part, the *secutor*, knowing that he had already wounded his enemy, decided to play a waiting game, hoping that the *retiarius*, by repeatedly thrusting at him with his trident, would increase the flow of blood from his injured leg. The crowd spotted this tactic immediately, and began to hurl abuse at the *secutor*. This was not fair, they shouted to each other, the man should fight instead of cowering behind his shield like a dog. Where was his courage? they screamed. Fight! came the cry from all around the *cavea*. Fight! Fight!

Having delayed as long as he dared (in view of the crowd's mood), the *secutor* decided to move on his opponent, thrusting his shield forward in an effort to catch the *retiarius* and throw him off balance. Alternating between thrusts of shield and sword, the *secutor* edged forward, as his opponent jabbed back with his trident. In this manner the two fighters slowly moved across the arena's short axis.

The crowd was now more on the side of the net-man than the pursuer, whose shameful stalling had lost him quite a few admirers. As each man continued to thrust and parry, they at last approached the marble *podium*. The *retiarius* glanced again at his wounded leg, wishing for some miracle to stem the steady drip of blood that was now congealing and caking around his calf. With every movement he could feel the thin coating tug at the hairs on his shin. Whenever he dodged a sword thrust or jabbed with his own weapon, he felt a stab of pain as salty sweat trickled into the wound.

The quality of the sounds issuing from behind him told the *retiarius* that he was near to the *podium*, so he moved to his right to allow himself more room. As he did so, he began a different line of attack. Now he stretched up high and jabbed at the *secutor* from above. When the other man brought his shield up to protect himself, the *retiarius* immediately crouched low and tried to thrust his trident underneath the shield. This strategy was costly, both in energy and in the blood that was squeezed from his leg wound with each extreme movement. The *retiarius* had no choice, however: he could feel himself starting to weaken from blood loss. He would have to defeat the *secutor* soon to have any hope of survival (true enough, the *secutor* had sacrificed his popularity with his stalling tactic, and this might well make the spectators merciful if the net-man fell; but the

final word did not rest with them – it rested with the Emperor
. . . it rested with Commodus . . .). The *retiarius* renewed his
attacks with all his remaining might.

The battle continued like this for a while longer, the *retiarius*
hoping that the *secutor* would soon be worn out by constantly
raising and dropping his shield, hoping that he would weaken
before the blood loss forced the *retiarius* to adopt another tactic.
As he defended himself against the constant up and down
thrusts of the trident, the *secutor* sought in vain the right
moment to counter-attack with his sword.

Presently, the shield grew slower in its continued rising and
falling. Finally, it rose too slowly to prevent the trident's prongs
from gouging three furrows in the *secutor*'s left shoulder. The
retiarius imagined the grimace that must have burst upon his
enemy's face, and he kept this image firmly in his mind as he
resolutely continued his assault. Every time the shield dropped,
he could glimpse more blood oozing from the torn shoulder. If
he intensified his attack now, he might be able to bring the
secutor down . . .

His leg was now throbbing with a pain that penetrated right
through to the bone. He felt himself growing steadily weaker.
He suddenly remembered that he had wounded the *secutor*'s *left*
shoulder, that his enemy's sword arm was as powerful as ever.
Surely it would be only a matter of seconds before the sword
was able to find its mark in this close-quarters conflict?

As soon as he had made the decision, the *retiarius* acted upon
it. Backing swiftly away, he turned and ran as fast as he could
back towards the net that lay abandoned on the far side of the
arena. The *secutor*, understanding instantly what was happening, stood up and gave desperate chase, casting his shield aside
as an encumbrance.

The *retiarius* now ran with his mind as much as his body; the
instinct for survival had fully taken over and was now at least as
important as his straining leg muscles. As he drew nearer to the

net, he could hear the panting of the *secutor* behind him, amplified by the great metal helmet. He did not dare look back: his thigh had already started to pump blood; what had begun as a steady and dangerous flow had become like a torrent as more veins had been torn by his exertions. His tunic was stained with blood and sweat and fell almost completely from his torso as he threw himself at the net.

The crowd jumped to their feet as the *retiarius* gathered up the weapon from which he took his name, swung it around in a single movement and hurled it at the on-rushing *secutor*. He raised his arms, but the defensive posture was useless: the net tangled itself about his legs and waist, and brought him crashing to the ground. A single triumphant scream rose from 50,000 throats as the *retiarius*, half dead himself, lifted his trident high above his head and prepared to plunge it into his adversary's chest.

At that moment, the *secutor* raised his left arm and presented his index finger to the *retiarius*, to the spectators, to the Emperor. The meaning was clear: in his final moment of life, the *secutor* decided to make a plea for mercy, to be allowed to leave the arena alive, so that he might fight again on another day, and perhaps be victorious.

The *retiarius* allowed his trident to fall to the sand, stood back and waited on unsteady legs for the verdict of the crowd. It was not favourable: the *secutor* had lost their support with his earlier attempt to avoid fighting his wounded opponent. Their gesture meant death. The *retiarius* looked up at the Emperor's box. But Commodus was not looking at him; he was gazing with glassy eyes at the fallen *secutor*. With a sneer and a cruelly arched eyebrow, he too gave the gesture for death.

There was now only one thing left for the *secutor* to do: in the manner in which he faced death he might at least restore some of the honour he had so foolishly thrown away early in the conflict, when he had every chance of emerging victorious.

Slowly, he pulled the net from about his legs, and drew himself to a half-kneeling posture. The *retiarius* picked up his opponent's fallen sword and approached him. As the *secutor* gripped the victor's thigh, the *retiarius* held his helmeted head in his left hand, and with his right plunged the sword through the neck of the vanquished. In the time-honoured manner of the defeated gladiator, the *secutor* did not flinch from the blade, nor did he make a sound as he died.

As was the custom, an attendant dressed as Charon, ferryman to the underworld, entered the arena, approached the *secutor*'s body and struck it with a mallet, signifying his ownership of the corpse. Following him strode another attendant, dressed as Mercury, shepherder of souls. He carried a *caduceus*, which was actually a red-hot iron, with which he prodded the body. Next, a group of stretcher-bearers approached, placed him on the stretcher and carried him away from the arena through the Porta Libitinaria, and into the *spoliarium*, in which his armour would be stripped from him.

The victorious gladiator then stepped up to the Emperor's box to receive his reward. On this occasion, Commodus presented him with the traditional symbol of victory, the palm leaf, and several gold coins. The *retiarius* then took his prizes and made a single victory circuit of the arena, to the shouts and applause of the spectators, before making his exit. He would not be required to fight again for several months.

Commodus found himself still out of sorts as the next two gladiators entered the arena. Try as he might, he could not rid himself of the feeling of annoyance caused by the wretch who had smiled up at him this morning. He watched the battles that followed with only vague interest; the struggles between the two-sword-wielding *dimachaeri*, the heavily-armoured *hoplomachi*, the chariot-riding *essedarii*, and the *laquearii* with their lethal lassos all left him completely unmoved. When a *murmillo* cleaved the skull of a *retiarius*, he merely yawned; when a *sagittarius* let fly his arrow with the utmost skill, felling his *samnis* opponent, Commodus sighed heavily and regarded his fingernails.

There was nothing else for it, he concluded: he would have to lift his spirits by taking to the arena himself. He was too far away from the blood and sand, the fighting and the death. He would have to do some killing himself, to drink in the adulation of the crowd even as the sand drank the spilled blood of his fallen opponents. As soon as he had decided, Commodus began to feel better; he even took an interest in the battles raging beneath him once more. Presently, he stood and left Emperor's platform.

Most of the spectators immediately knew what was about to happen as they saw the Emperor stand and slip quickly from his platform. Word spread throughout the *cavea* almost instantly, so that even those who had been concentrating on the battles on the arena floor, thus missing his unceremonious exit, now knew that the Emperor was about to fight. In the maze of cells and passageways beneath the amphitheatre, the remaining gladiators cast their eyes down with a barely perceptible slumping of the shoulders. They knew that those who would be called upon to fight the Emperor would not be doing so with real weapons, but with the *rudis*, the wooden sword, the useless toy, the guarantor of death.

When the last battle had been fought, the arena was again cleansed of blood and other debris. When the Emperor entered through the great arch on the arena's long axis, the orchestra let fly with an elaborate flourish, and the crowd cheered deafeningly and stood as one. Commodus strode to the centre of the great space and waved to his people. His sumptuous clothes had already been exchanged for a simple tunic. His weapon was a single *gladius*; in truth, it was the only weapon he would need, although there were others near the *podium*, should he grow bored with it and decide to use another.

The knights and senators watching from above knew their lines well, for Commodus had taken to the arena on countless previous occasions. As the Emperor rushed at his first opponent, a *dimachaerus* armed with two wooden swords, and plunged his own blade deep into the man's chest, the knights and senators all shouted the oft-recited *paean*: 'Thou art lord and thou art first! Of all men most fortunate! Victor thou art! And victor thou shalt be! From everlasting, Amazonian, thou art victor!'

These words rang out again and again, and mingled with the roar of the other spectators, as Commodus strode from one end of the arena to the other and back again, thrusting and hacking with his sword, taking off heads and arms, slicing legs and torsos, the moans of the dying fading in his wake. Gladiators of all kinds fell before him, and after an hour or so, he began to weary, so he stopped, rested on his *gladius* and beckoned to a slave girl waiting by the *podium*. She came forward, carrying a golden goblet in the shape of a mace. Commodus took the goblet from her and drank deep of the cool, honeyed wine which it contained.

Then, it was back to work. More slaughter, more cheers, more praise, more blood. At one point, Commodus spied a knight who did not seem to be cheering with the same degree of rapture as his fellows. Throwing down his sword, the Emperor strode across the arena to the *podium*, took his bow and a single arrow and let it fly through the heart of the insolent knight. Without so much as a glance at his lifeless body, his fellows redoubled their efforts to show their appreciation of their Emperor's gladiatorial skills.

Finally, as the sun sank low upon the horizon, and the Emperor had at last sated his own bloodlust, the day's games drew to a close. There was, however, one final battle to be waged – one that had nothing to do with gladiators or beasts. Many of the spectators chose this time to vacate their seats and leave the amphitheatre, not having the stomach – or the brute strength – for what was to follow. It was time for the *sparsio*. The crowd stopped their cheering, sat down, and waited as a catapult-like machine called a *linea* was brought into the arena.

This machine contained hundreds of tokens, each representing a gift from the Emperor to his people. The value of these gifts was wide-ranging, and included everything from a brace of birds for a plebeian's table, to a country house.

The struggle that ensued as the *linea* flung the tokens among the tiers was almost as bloody as the gladiatorial combats that had preceded it. The reason was simple enough: within the howling mob were many plebeians who had borrowed money against a pledge of the prizes they were pursuing. Others had taken a fixed sum from a speculator, and had pledged themselves to hand over every token they could grab.

Commodus, in the meantime, had returned to the Emperor's platform, and watched with great amusement the plebeians around him as they kicked and punched each other, tore hair out and trod on prone bodies in their desperate attempts to grab a valuable token. Like ravenous dogs they scrambled across the tiers, covered with blood, their own and others', nursing broken noses and arms, their wounds barely noticed as they flung themselves upon the booty. This was how the day at the games ended. The violence and degradation of the arena had spread, as usual, throughout the amphitheatre.

CHAPTER THIRTEEN

The End of a Cruel Era

XIII

The abolition of gladiatorial contests was not achieved in a single day, or even a single year. It was very much a piecemeal affair, with occasional edicts being issued by Emperors in response to a very gradual growth in opposition. The first of these edicts was issued by the Emperor Constantine the Great.

Constantine the Great, whose full name was Flavius Valerius Constantinus, was born in Nis (in what is now the former Yugoslavia) about AD 274, and was Roman Emperor from 306–37. He was the first Roman ruler to be converted to Christianity, and was the founder of the city of Constantinople (now Istanbul), which was the capital of the Eastern Roman (Byzantine) Empire until 1453.

His father was the commander Constantius Chlorus (later Constantius I), and his mother was named Helena (later Saint Helena, who is said to have found the True Cross on which Jesus was crucified in the Holy Land). Constantine was very popular with his troops (he joined his father in Britain in 306), who proclaimed him Emperor when Constantius died later that year. However, Constantine had to struggle constantly with his rivals for about 20 years before he was able to establish himself as sole ruler in 324.

It was on the eve of a battle with one of his rivals, Maxentius, that Constantine (a pagan sun-worshipper) is said to have dreamed that Christ appeared to him and instructed him to inscribe the first two letters of his name (XP in Greek) on the shields of his soldiers. The following day, he saw a cross on the sun, and the words 'in hoc signo vinces' ('in this sign you will be the victor'). He went on to defeat Maxentius at the Battle of the Milvian Bridge, near Rome.

As a result of his vision, Constantine ended persecution of the Christians with his Edict of Milan in 313. His other reforms included the separation of civil and military authority, and the reorganisation of the army. His great achievement was to unify the crumbling Empire, reorganised the state and made possible the final victory of Christianity at the end of the fourth century

The first of his edicts about gladiators was issued in Beirut in AD 325. Addressed to the Praetorian Prefect Maximus, Vicar of the Oriens (Egypt and the Asiatic provinces), the edict stated:

> In an age of public peace and domestic tranquillity, spectacles involving the shedding of blood displease us. We therefore utterly forbid the existence of gladiators; ensure that those persons who, because of their crimes, used to be sentenced to become gladiators, should now be sentenced to the mines, so that they can pay the penalty for their criminal behaviour without having to shed their blood.

However, the abolition of the games was not enforced for some time: in fact, Constantine himself allowed municipal priests in Umbria to continue to give gladiatorial shows, and instructed that such shows should be concentrated at the Etrurian religious centre, Volsinii (Orvieto). Some years earlier, Constantine had condemned kidnappers to gladiatorial schools:

> Kidnappers who inflict on parents the lamentable bereavement of their living children were formerly sentenced to the mines or other similar punishments. In future, if any person is charged with such a crime and his guilt is manifest, then if he is a slave or freedman he shall be thrown to the wild beasts at

the next public spectacle; but if he is freeborn, he shall be handed to a gladiatorial school under the proviso that before he does anything to escape punishment, he shall be destroyed by the sword.

In spite of the fact that the Church declared that gladiators, their *lanistae* and those organising wild-beast displays could not be baptised, the December games were still given by the quaestors at Rome as late as AD 354.

But gradually, more legislation against gladiatorial combats was put in place. In 357 Constantius II issued an edict that Roman officials should not take part in gladiatorial games. In 365 and 367, Valentinian I forbade the condemnation of Christians to fight as gladiators. The last gladiatorial contest in an eastern province probably took place at Antioch in around 392. Eight years later, the Emperor Honorius closed the last gladiatorial schools at Rome.

The early opposition to gladiatorial contests was not initially based on revulsion at the idea of men killing each other, or being torn to pieces by wild beasts. It is interesting to look at the attitude of Tertullian, the first important Christian ecclesiastical writer in Latin.

Tertullian (AD 160? – 220?), trained as a lawyer and practised at Rome until some time between 190 and 195, when he was converted to Christianity. After visiting Greece and Asia Minor, he returned to Carthage in 197 and became a presbyter of the Church. In around 207, he became the leader of an ascetic sect known as the Montanists, which was known for its prophesying. As a result of their increasing conflict with Church authorities, the Montanists were eventually declared heretical.

Thirty-one of Tertullian's theological treatises have survived, in which his attitudes to ethics, discipline and morality become increasingly harsh with time. Were it not for his support of the Montanists, Tertullian would have been considered one of the great Fathers of the Church. Nevertheless, his influence upon the Church was considerable, and many of his ideas are considered orthodox by Roman Catholicism.

Tertullian's most famous work is the *Apologeticus* (c. 197), in which he defends the Christians against the charges of political subversion, immorality and economic worthlessness that were levelled against them. Elsewhere in his work, he refutes heresy, claiming that only the Church has the authority to decide what is and is not orthodox Christianity. He also exhorted Christians not to attend gladiatorial and other public shows.

His method of attacking spectacles was to divide them into three categories: chariot-racing, gladiatorial contests and theatrical shows. The first he describes as 'mad', the second 'savage' and the third 'titillating'. However, when he attacks the gladiatorial contests as 'savage', he is not referring to the violent and bloody nature of the combats themselves, but rather to the emotions they aroused in the spectators. In the mid-third century, the writer Minucius Felix used the same division of spectacles as Tertullian, but with a different intention. Instead of 'savage', he described gladiatorial contests as 'manslaughter', thus shifting the criticism from the emotions experienced by the spectators to the activity itself.

The Church fathers expressed serious concerns about the damage that might be sustained by the Christian soul while viewing gladiatorial combats. Of these, Augustine was particularly vocal. Born in AD 354 in Tagaste, Numidia (now Souk-Ahras, Algeria), he was the greatest of the Latin Fathers and one of the most highly respected Western Doctors of the Church. His education as a rhetorician was conducted in the North African cities of Tagaste, Madaura and Carthage. Augustine lived with a Carthaginian woman (whose name is not known) between the ages of 15 and 30, with whom he had a son. He named the boy Adeodatus, which means 'gift of God'.

Inspired by the writings of Cicero, Augustine devoted himself to a search for truth; this led him ultimately to enter the Church. Between 373 and 382 he followed the doctrine of Manichaeism, which was popular in the Western Roman Empire at the time. This Persian dualistic philosophy was based upon the concept of the eternal struggle between good and evil, which struck Augustine as the most plausible principle on which to base an ethical system. Augustine was attracted to Manichaeism partly because its moral code was not stifling or unpalatably censorious: the famous line 'Give me chastity and continence, but not just now' is Augustine's.

From Carthage he moved to Rome around 383, and from there went to Milan, where he studied Neoplatonism, met the Bishop of Milan, Saint Ambrose, and embraced Christianity after hearing a voice saying: 'Take up and read.' This he interpreted as an instruction to read the Scriptures.

After returning to North Africa and being ordained in 391, he became Bishop of Hippo (now Annaba, Algeria) in 395, and held the office until his death in 430. During this time, he concentrated on the battle between theological doctrines that was raging within the Church. Two of the conflicts involved a sect known as the Donatists, who refused to acknowledge the sacraments unless they were administered by sinless ecclesiastics, and the Pelagians, who denied the doctrine of original sin.

Augustine's doctrines (including those of original sin, divine grace and predestination), which occupied the middle ground between Pelagianism and Manichaeism, were immensely influential in the development of Christianity, Roman Catholic and Protestant alike.

A prolific writer, his best-known work is the *Confessions* (c. 400) an autobiography dealing with his early life and conversion to Christianity. It is in this work that he describes the perversion of morality he witnessed in one of his fellow students at Carthage in the 360s, after attending a gladiatorial show:

When he saw the blood, it was as though he had drunk a deep draught of savage passion. Instead of turning away, he fixed his eyes upon the scene and drank in all its frenzy, unaware of what he was doing. He revelled in the wickedness of the fighting and was drunk with the fascination of bloodshed.

His student colleague thus was afflicted with 'a diseased mind' that would allow him no rest until he had returned to the amphitheatre. Whereas before he had been cajoled by his friends into going, now he cajoled others, 'leading new sheep to the slaughter'.

For Augustine, gladiatorial combats represented an utterly useless and dangerous diversion from the serious concerns of life, both material and spiritual. He also concentrated on the ambivalent attitude of Romans to the gladiators: that curious mixture of utter contempt and breathless adulation. Augustine pointed out the absurdity of this attitude: surely it was ridiculous that a group identified so closely with slaves and prostitutes should be the object of any serious person's attention.

The historian Thomas Wiedemann points to the complex attitudes of Christians to the cruelty of the games, noting that the surviving literary sources 'see the moral problem of cruelty from the point of view of the Christian who may have to witness or even inflict it, not that of the convict or gladiator who suffers it'. Around 403, when the poet Prudentius denounced the pagan Symmachus (who had spoken most unsympathetically of the Saxon prisoners who had killed each other rather than appear at the *munus* he had organised), he maintained that forcing criminals to perform as gladiators should no longer be allowed. However, this can hardly have been the result of a humanitarian sensibility, since he went on to say that criminals should be thrown to the beasts instead.

Shortly after this, around the year 404, came an event that was to prove highly significant to attitudes towards gladiatorial combat. It involved a monk from Asia Minor named Telemachus, who ran into a Roman arena to prevent a battle between two gladiators. The crowd was so outraged that they immediately seized the hapless Telemachus and literally tore him to pieces. In response to this, the Emperor Honorius took the opportunity to ban gladiators and gladiatorial games altogether. However, this ban did not apply throughout the Empire; nor was it permanent at Rome. Wiedemann suggests that it was most likely a temporary punishment, much like that imposed upon the people of Pompeii by Nero after the riots that broke out there in AD 59. He continues: 'As late as the AD 430s or 440s, *contorniates* (medallions commemorating the holders of consulships) depict gladiators in combat; one from 410 or later is inscribed "May the restoration of the *munus* have a happy outcome."'

There are no further known references to gladiators, although that does not prove that such combats ceased altogether. Theatrical performances, chariot-races and *venationes* are mentioned, but regarding gladiatorial shows, there is silence. As Wiedemann notes: 'Western Church councils in the fifth century do not repeat the threats of excommunication against gladiators which are found in Augustine.' They also vanish from the literary sources, such as the poems of the *Codex Salmasianus*, and documents regarding the giving of public games, which include chariot-races and *venationes*.

About one hundred years after Prudentius, in the eastern empire, Anastasius I forbade contests between men and beasts, but allowed fights between beasts to continue. In the years following the last of the western Emperors, the Ostrogothic ruler Theoderic denounced the throwing of criminals to beasts in 523.

The part played by Christianity in the abolition of gladiatorial contests is not quite as straightforward as might be assumed. While the spreading of Christian ideas did ultimately result in the disappearance of the gladiators, the final abolition had little to do with the unacceptability of such cruelty, or even the pagan origin and nature of gladiatorial *munera*. According to Wiedemann, 'the Christian society of late antiquity no longer needed them as a symbol of the dividing line between who belonged and who did not: as the means by which the outsider can enter, or re-enter, respectable society'. The *munus* had been replaced by the sacrament of baptism. In addition, Roman society could no longer consider itself entirely separate from north-western Europe. When barbarians began to be assimilated into the Roman army, the practise of forcing them into gladiatorial schools became somewhat superfluous.

The early centuries of Christianity display little in the way of compassion, at least on the part of the Emperors. In fact, in Christian Rome and Byzantium, wild-beast displays were swiftly integrated into society and stripped of their pagan associations. The Byzantine Emperor Prudentius considered it quite acceptable to throw criminals to the beasts, and even claimed that any city in which this happened would be devoted to God. From Constantine on, the range of crimes punishable by fire or beast was actually extended, although it may be that such legislation was enacted merely to provide the Emperor with the opportunity to display the virtue of clemency.

What is clear is that early Christianity had no problem whatsoever with cruelty to animals and humans. Thomas Wiedemann explains the evidence:

> The ivory diptych advertising the consular games of Aerobindus in AD 506 shows, on one of its leaves, the crowd in the Circus at Constantinople watching acrobats baiting bears, and on the other four *bestiarii* despatching lions with their spears in much the same poses as on representations four centuries earlier.

To the pagan Roman mind, the destruction of a wild beast represented the power of Rome over the chaotic forces of Nature. To the Christian mind, the analogy was altered, so that the beast came to represent not only the natural world which had to be tamed in order to attain salvation, but also the vices and passions within oneself which it was essential to subdue and conquer.

For the Christian, the most serious problem presented by gladiatorial combats was not that they involved the bloody and agonising slaughter of men; it was that they resulted in a form of resurrection that had nothing to do with the Christian God. In pagan Roman eyes, the gladiator (in spite of the adulation he received from the public) was *infamis*, occupying the very lowest level of society; and yet, by the nature of his profession, he was offered the chance of regaining his *virtus* by displaying skill and bravery in the arena. The salvation thus offered by gladiatorial combat was unacceptable to Christianity, since it was offered not by God, but by the Roman people. For this reason, as much as for the principle of Christian brotherly kindness, the practice of gladiatorial combat could not continue.

Today the amphitheatres are silent. The horror of the gladiatorial combats has been gone for centuries, the fighters and speactators have long since turned to dust and on the ruined arena floors, where the blood of men and beasts once flew, peace has returned.

Glossary

GLOSSARY

ANDABATE: A type of gladiator who was fully armoured, and who wore a helmet without eye-holes. They usually charged blindly at each other on horseback.

AUCTORATUS: A man who has taken the gladiator's oath.

BESTIARIUS: A professional fighter of wild beasts; also a criminal condemned to face the beasts unarmed.

CATASTA: A platform reached by a ramp, upon which *retiarii* occasionally fought.

CAVEA: the tiers of an amphitheatre.

COCHLEA: A rotating mechanism made of wood, and used to confuse attacking animals during a *venatio*.

CONFECTOR: An arena attendant who killed wounded animals.

DIMACHAERUS: A type of gladiator who carried a short sword in each hand.

DOCTOR: The weapons instructor for gladiators. He specialised in the use of certain weapons, and was often an ex-gladiator.

EDITOR: The person who paid for and presided over a *munus*. In the early years of the games, he could be a private individual, such as a magistrate; but later the role was taken over by the Emperor.

ESSEDARIUS: A type of gladiator who fought from a chariot.

FAMILIA GLADIATORIA: The name given to a troupe of gladiators, all of whom were owned by the *lanista*.

AD FLAMMAS: A method of execution by burning.

GALERUS: A piece of metal that protected the left shoulder of a *retiarius* or a *laquearius*.

GALLUS: The pre-Augustan term for a *murmillo*.

GAMES: Official spectacles that were given free to the Roman population. Originally a celebration of the life of an illustrious person following his funeral, subsequently they were held for their own sake.

GREGATIM: Gladiatorial battles in which a large number of fighters take part at once.

HARENARIUS: Legal term for a criminal sentenced to fight in the arena.

HONESTIORES: The privileged classes of late antiquity.

HOPLOMACHUS: A type of gladiator armed with a long, oblong shield; possibly also a gladiator who was completely covered with armour.

LANISTA: The owner of a gladiatorial troupe, responsible for their training. He rented his troupe to the *editor* of the games.

LAQUEARIUS: A type of gladiator who used a lasso.

LIBELLUS NUMERARIUS: A programme, sold in the streets prior to a *munus*, listing the names of the gladiators who were to fight.

LUDI: (a) Festivals in honour of various divinities; (b) Gladiatorial training schools.

AD LUDOS: Judicial penalty of a period of three years as a gladiator, followed by two more years of imprisonment.

MANICA: A piece of leather, reinforced with metal scales, that protected the sword arm of a gladiator.

MISSIO: The decision to allow a gladiator who had fought bravely, but had been defeated, to leave the arena alive.

MISSUS: Term applied to a gladiator who had been allowed to live following a defeat.

MUNUS, pl. MUNERA: An obligatory gift, something 'owed', as a funeral is owed to the deceased. Subsequently, the contribution of gladiatorial games made by a citizen to his community.

MURMILLO: The post-Augustan word for a *Gallus*. This gladiator was heavily armed with a rectangular shield and a visored helmet with a fish-shaped crest. He normally fought a *retiarius*.

NAUMACHIA: From the time of Caesar onwards, a naval display which included gladiatorial battles.

OCREA: A greave, or piece of leg armour, protecting the lower leg. On the Thracians, this armour also covered the knee.

PALUS: Wooden training stake upon which gladiators practised their fighting skills.

POMPA: The ceremonial parade preceding the spectacles, accompanied by music.

PROBATIO ARMORUM: The inspection of weapons by the president of the games.

RETIARIUS: A type of gladiator who wore only a light tunic and fought with a net and trident. He usually fought either a *murmillo* or a *secutor.*

RUDIS (also SUMMA RUDIS): A wooden sword used in training, and also the symbol of freedom presented to a gladiator on his release from service.

SAGITTARIUS: A type of gladiator who fought with a bow.

SAMNIS, pl. SAMNITES: The pre-Augustan term for a *secutor.*

SECUTOR: A type of gladiator who carried a rectangular shield, a visored helmet, greaves and a *manica.*

SILVAE: Spectacles in which animals were hunted in an artificial woodland setting within the arena.

SINE MISSIONE: A fight to the death. Even if the defeated gladiator had fought well and bravely, he was automatically denied the possibility of life.

SPOLIARIUM: The hall in which defeated gladiators were stripped of their arms. It was reached by means of the 'mortuary door' on the long axis of the arena, opposite the door through which gladiators entered.

STANS: A term describing a combat in which there was no clear victory.

SUPPOSITICIUS: A gladiator who entered the arena at the end of a battle, and whom the victor was forced to face immediately.

THRAEX: A type of gladiator who fought in the Thracian style, with a round shield and a curved short sword.

TIRO: A trainee gladiator.

VELARIUM: A vast awning designed to shield the spectators from the sun.

VELES: A type of gladiator who fought with a javelin.

VENABULUM: A spear-like weapon, reinforced with an iron point, used by *venatores* to fight beasts.

VENATIONES: Animal hunts, in which beasts of all kinds were killed in the arena.

VENATORES: Another term for *bestiarii.*

Bibliography
and Suggested
Further Reading

There are few books on the subject of gladiators, gladiatorial combat and wild-beast shows. For those readers wishing to study these subject a little further, I strongly recommend the work of Auguet, Grant and Wiedemann, which I found extremely helpful in preparing this book. Also listed are a number of other books which provided useful information, together with a collection of websites containing good information on this and related subjects.

BOOKS:

Auguet, Roland: *Cruelty and Civilization*. London: Routledge, 1998.

Freeman, Charles: *Egypt, Greece and Rome: Civilisations of the Ancient Mediterranean*. Oxford: Oxford University Press, 1996.

Barton, Carlin: *The Sorrows of the Ancient Romans: The Gladiator and the Monster*. Princeton, New Jersey: Princeton University Press, 1993.

Futrell, Alison: *Blood in the Arena: The Spectacle of Roman Power*. Austin, Texas: Austin University Press, 1997.

Grant, Michael: *Nero*. London: Weidenfeld & Nicolson, 1970.

Grant, Michael: *Gladiators*. London: Penguin Books, 2000.

Hopkins, Keith: *Death and Renewal*. Cambridge: Cambridge University Press, 1983.

Hornblower, Simon and Spawforth, Antony (eds.): *Oxford Classical Dictionary*, third edition. Oxford: Oxford University Press, 1996.

Meier, Christian: *Julius Caesar*. London: HarperCollins Publishers, 1995.

Petronius: *The Satyricon*. London: Penguin Books, 1986.

Plutarch: *Fall of the Roman Republic*. London: Penguin Books, 1972.

Seneca: *The Apocolocyntosis*. London: Penguin Books, 1986.

Suetonius: *The Twelve Caesars*. London: Penguin Books, 1989.

Tacitus: *The Annals of Imperial Rome*. London: Penguin Books, 1996.

Wiedemann, Thomas: *Emperors and Gladiators*. London: Routledge, 1996.

WEBSITES:

Gladiatorial Games
http://www.vroma.org/~bmcmanus/arena.html
RomanSites
http://www.ukans.edu/history/index/europe/ancient_rome/E/Roman/RomanSites*/home.html
Barbara F. McManus Classics Pages
http://www.cnr.edu/home/bmcmanus/
LacusCurtius: Into the Roman World
http://www.ukans.edu/history/index/europe/ancient_rome/E/Roman/home.html
Roman Gladiatorial Games
http://depthome.brooklyn.cuny.edu/classics/gladiatr/index.htm

Index

INDEX

INDEX

the five categories of, 18

sponsorship and, 35, 36–7, 72

as symbols of Rome, 39, 80

stage effects for, 78–9

death during, 84–6, 145–8

account of, 183–4

abolition of, 197–205

and salvation, 205

Gladiator school. *See Ludus*

Gladiators

life expectancy of, 3, 10

and death, 19

social origins of, 20

recruitement of, 20–1, 43

advantages to being, 21–3, 46–7

as love objects, 22–5, 25–7

status of, 29, 52, 115, 205

oath of joining, 44

training of, 45–6

wages of, 46–7

cost of, 47–50

life of, 50–2

types of, 53–7

combat and, 84–6, 92

emperors who fought as, 115–25, 192–3

fighting achievements of, 183–4

Gladiators' insurrection (73BC), 61–6

Gladius, 12

Grant, Michael, 3, 55, 72, 79, 142

Great Fire of Rome (AD 64), 141, 144

Gregatim, 92

Hadrian, Emperor, 50, 115, 130

Halicarnassus, 27

Hannibal, 15

Hermes, 46

Hierocles, 26–7

Historia Augusta, 40, 130

Historia Naturalis, 70

Honestiores, 130

Honorius, Emperor, 199, 203

Hoplomachus, 53

Horace, 91

Human sacrifice, 11, 12, 26

Humiliores, 130

Jupiter Optimus Maximus, 15

Justice, the games and, 39–40, 80

Juvenal, 17, 23–4, 28, 56

Kidnapping, 198–9

Lanista, 20, 21, 44, 46, 48–9, 50, 57, 83

Laquearii, 53

Legion I Minervia, 109

Lentulus, Consul, 64

Lepidus, Marcus Aemilius, 90

Leptinus, Furius, 34

Letters, 37

Libellus Numerarius, 158, 183

Libitina, 83, 86

Life of Crassus, 61

Linea, 194

Lituus, 83

Lives of the Caesars, 27

Livy, 15, 91

Longinus, Gaius Cassius, 91

Lucilla, 123

Lucillius, 147

Ludi, 14–16

Ludus, 25, 43, 44, 45, 46

imperial, 44, 49

life in, 50–7

closing of, 199

Ludus Dacicus, 49

Ludus Gallicus, 49

Ludus Magnus, 49–50

Ludus Matutinus, 49

Lyons, 132

Magistri, 100, 102

Manicae, 55

Marius, Gaius, 33

Martial, 45–6, 89, 135, 146

Marx, Karl, 64

Maxentius, 197–8

Meier, Christian, 64

Menageries, 109–110

Meniscus, 147

Mercy, requests for, 84

Messalina, 135–6

Missio, 40, 46, 85

Missiones passivae, 104

Montanus, 142

Moral Essays, 52

Munus, 10–12, 13, 16–23, 34, 35–7, 48,

INDEX

INDEX